12 TH EDITION

CALIFORNIA

MARRIAGE

LAW

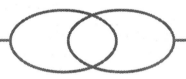

by California attorneys

ED SHERMAN

& Lorie Leigh Robertson

Nolo Press - Occidental

SPECIAL THANKS
to Ralph Warner, Toni Ihara and Stephen Elias
who nurtured this book from 1976 through 1992

TWELFTH EDITION
First Printing   April 1995
Legal Research   LORIE LEIGH ROBERTSON
Illustrations   MARI STEIN
Typography   STEPHEN POLLARD
Printing   DIVERSIFIED PRINTERS, BREA, CA

Although great care has been taken to ensure the accuracy and utility of the information and forms contained in this book, no warranty is made, express or implied, and neither Nolo Press nor the authors assume any liability in connection with any use or result from use of the information or forms contained herein.

ISBN 0-944508-21-9
Library of Congress No. 80-11750

Legal research and the footnotes

This book gives you a good overview of California law, but if you want to know more about a subject, you can look in your local law library where you can find the code sections and cases we've referred to in the footnotes. Call your county offices and ask for the law library nearest you.

Finding code sections is easy; just get the book of codes referred to and look up the section cited. Finding cases takes more guidance. Show the citation to the librarian and ask for help.

Case citations: the meaning of the numbers. California Supreme Court decisions are published in the *Official Reports of the California Supreme Court* (called "California Reports") and Appellate Court decisions are in the *Official Reports of the California Courts of Appeal* (called "California Appellate Reports).

Case citations in the footnotes are a shorthand code for where a case can be found—it's location in a numbered volume in numbered series of volumes at a particular page. It works like this:

> *Marvin vs. Marvin* (1976) 18 C3d 660 means that the case of Marvin vs. Marvin (decided in 1976) can be found in volume 18 of the California Reports, third series, at page 660.

In this abbreviation system C = California Reports; C2d is the second series; C3d is the third series, and so on. CA = California Appellate Reports; CA2d is the second series; CA3d is the third series, and so on.

To go beyond reading cases and statutes in the footnotes, you should learn some basic legal research techniques. Read Nolo's *Legal Research: How to Find and Understand the Law*, by Steve Elias. You can learn a lot from legal encyclopedias and commentaries. Here are some good ones commonly used by attorneys: *Summary of California Law*, 9th edition, by Bernard Witkin (Bancroft-Whitney); *California Practice Guide (Family Law)* by Hogoboom and King (The Rutter Group); and *California Family Law Reports*, by Adams & Sevitch.

Related Nolo Press books
—see inside front cover and back of this book

In the text, we often refer you to other good Nolo Press books that go into some subject in much greater detail. Descriptions of these books and order information can be found at the inside front cover and in the back of this book. Please note that the books in the front are ordered from a different place than the books listed in the back.

Table of contents

1 ♦ The "not really married" relationship

2 ◆ Getting married—read the small print

3 ◆ Yours, mine and ours—the community property system

4 ◆ Debts: Who owes what?

5 ◆ Marriage and pre-marriage contracts

6 ◆ Children

7 ◆ Child rearing by separated parents

8 ◆ Is my family provided for? Estate planning

9 ◆ Domestic violence

10 ◆ Divorce—how to reduce pain and cost

1

The "not really married" relationship

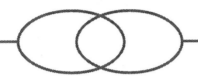

The term "marriage" means different things to different people. Some feel that marriage is the union of spirit and soul; the ultimate commitment. Others feel that "marriage" is whatever people in a relationship want it to be.

In this book the term "marriage" will only refer to those relationships where a valid legal marriage exists as defined by California law. Whether or not the legal definition of marriage is too narrow (it surely must be) will not be discussed. Most of this book concerns the marital relationship (the valid legal marriage). But first, this chapter discusses a important things you should know about the unmarried relationship. If you find you want to know even more, see Nolo's *The Living Together Kit*.

A. A little about the *Marvin* case

You may have heard about the famous legal battle of *Marvin vs. Marvin*.[1] Lee Marvin and Michele Triola lived together for about 7 years and then split up. Michele sued, claiming that she and Marvin had agreed orally to share all earnings and assets. She argued that she had given up a career as a singer to become Marvin's housekeeper, cook and companion, and that it would be unfair for Marvin to keep all the assets acquired during their relationship. The California Supreme Court agreed and held that a contract to split assets can be oral, implied by the parties' conduct or based upon the reasonable expectations of the parties' agreement to share equally in asset accumulation.

The Marvin case illuminates the point that couples who are not legally married will have

their claims against each other decided by standard contract law principles.

B. Understanding the nonmarital relationship

Nonmarital relationships are those where the legal requirements of a marriage have not been met. If you are wondering, "What possible difference can a piece of paper make?" you will soon find out that in the world of laws, money, debts and property, it makes a great deal of difference!

The nonmarital relationship includes:

• Couples who are precluded by law from a legal marriage (same-sex relationships, close relatives, etc.).

• Couples who have decided for any reason against getting legally married.

Bottom line: as far the law is concerned, either you are married—meaning you have met the legal requirements; or you are not— in which case your relationship is considered nonmarital in the halls of the courthouse.

Regardless of the type of nonmarital relationship you have, certain basic principles apply. It is important to understand them. Don't confuse the common law marriage (discussed in Chapter 2) with the nonmarital relationship. Legally they are different beasts so different rules apply.

C. What are my property rights?

When a couple lives together without the formalities of a legal marriage, California courts apply general contract law principles to decide any legal issues concerning the relationship. Nonmarital partners do not

---

[1] *Marvin vs. Marvin* (1976) 18 C3d 660

acquire the property rights that flow from marital status. This can be significant since California is a community property state, which means that marital relationships are governed by community property laws, and these laws provide parties to a valid legal marriage with important protections that are not afforded to parties in a nonmarital relationship. (We will explain the community property system in Chapter 3.)

One of the protections afforded by California community property law is the *presumption* that property acquired by either spouse during marriage is owned equally by both spouses. However, if a couple is only living together, no presumption of equal ownership exists. (If something is presumed, it is up to the other party to show clear evidence strong enough to overcome the presumption.)

Examples

Dick and Jane decide to marry and that Jane will quit her promising career and manage their home. Dick and Jane later decide to divorce. During the marriage, Dick was able to save $20,000 from his salary. Since Dick's salary is community property (because it is property acquired during marriage) Jane is entitled to half of the $20,000 Dick saved because it is owned equally by both spouses.

Sonny and Cher decide to live together and that Cher should quit her singing career in order to manage their household. While they lived together Sonny was able to save $30,000 from his singing gigs. They decide to split up and Cher asks for her half of the $30,000. Since they are not married, community property laws don't apply. So unless Cher can prove that she and Sonny had an agreement to share all assets acquired while they were living together, she will not be entitled to any of the $30,000.

Moral of the story: if you are not married it is *very* important to have a written agreement as to who owns what and other income and debt matters. If you have agreed with

your partner to share all income and assets acquired during your relationship, make sure you have a *written* agreement signed by your partner expressing those intentions!

D. Am I responsible for my partner's debts?

Generally, no. Your wages or property cannot be attached to pay your partner's bills. However, if you co-sign a loan, open a joint bank account or sign a credit agreement with your partner, you will become responsible for any debt or losses incurred in those accounts. Our advice: keep your finances separate. If you decide to buy a house or other large asset with your partner, make sure the title and loan documents accurately reflect your ownership interest.

E. What if we have children together?

No one ever doubts who a child's mother is, but with fathers it's not always so easy. By ancient legal tradition (begun centuries before DNA tracing) whenever a married woman has a child, the child is conclusively presumed to be her husband's child.[2] It takes powerful evidence to overcome this pre-

---

[2]Family Code §7540

sumption. But the presumption of paternity does not apply to nonmarital partners: for children born to an unmarried mother, the paternity of the child is an open question. *Paternity* simply means "fatherhood; the state, fact or condition of being a father." Since a host of rights and responsibilities flow from the parent-child relationship, it is important for nonmarital partners to clearly establish the paternity of any children.

To protect the father, the mother and the child, nonmarital partners who have a child *must* make a written paternity statement. This is a simple document, signed by the father and mother, which acknowledges that the child is theirs. Having a paternity statement can be vital if problems develop in the areas of inheritance, child support, visitation, guardianship or adoption. Sample paternity statements are available in Nolo's *The Living Together Kit*.

If you think filling out a paternity statement is unnecessary, think again. Paternity disputes are complicated, humiliating and expensive. Take the time to protect yourself and your child.

F. Medical emergencies

Married couples are empowered by law to make medical decisions for each other in situations where the injured or sick spouse has become unable to make his or her own decisions. However, if a member of an unmarried couple becomes seriously ill or disabled, medical authorities will be forced to turn to his or her parents, adult children or siblings to make medical decisions. The unmarried partner might even have trouble visiting. If you want your partner to make medical decisions for you, and vice versa, you must *each* prepare a "durable power of

attorney for health care." Samples of these documents can be found in *Nolo's Simple Will Book* and *Make Your Own Living Trust*.

A power of attorney is a document that allows one person (called the "principal") to delegate legal authority to another person (called the "attorney in fact") to act on his or her behalf. The document can be effective for a specific period of time or it can be drafted so that it remains in effect even after the *principal* has become incapacitated. When the power of attorney remains effective even after the incapacity of the *principal*, it is called a *durable* power of attorney.

Essentially, a durable power of attorney (whether it be financial or for health care), is designed to give someone the legal authority to make important financial and medical decisions for you or to implement decisions you have previously made, in the event you should become incapacitated. A durable power of attorney can be drafted so that it does not become effective until and *unless* you become incapacitated. This allows you to retain full control over your affairs unless you become unable to do so.

Taking the time to draft an appropriate durable power of attorney will allow *you* to decide how your affairs will be handled in the event of your incapacity. In addition, a durable power of attorney will be priceless to your loved ones; if you should become unable to handle your affairs, it will spare them infinite trouble, worry and expense.

G. Health insurance

Health insurance is a contractual benefit, which means that each policy has its own terms and conditions. To determine if your policy will cover your partner, contact the plan administrator. Increasingly companies

are allowing nonmarital partners to partici-pate in health care plans. But beware! Even if you pay the premiums but are not legally married, coverage can be denied if the policy's terms require that a valid marriage exist before extending coverage.

H. Can I take my partner's name?

In California, people over the age of eigh-teen have the right to assume the first, last and middle names of their choice. There are two valid legal ways to change your name in California; the *usage* method and by *petition-ing the court.*

You can take your partner's name by using the new name consistently (the usage method). When you use this method to change your name, no court action is neces-sary and the change is legally valid.[3] How-ever, for the name change to be valid you *must* use the new name consistently.

For a complete discussion on how to change your name, see Nolo's *How to Change Your Name*, by Loeb and Brown.

---

[3]Code of Civil Procedure §1279.5

I. Social Security, welfare and other government benefits

1. Social Security

Let's take Social Security first. This is one area where unmarried couples are certainly discriminated against. As a partner in an unmarried couple, you are only entitled to whatever benefits you individually earned. This differs importantly from married couples: the spouse of a wage earner who contributed to Social Security is eligible upon retirement to receive benefits based upon their spouse's contribution. A widower or a divorced spouse of a wage earner is also eligible for benefits.

If you and your partner are able (under California law) to get married and you have chosen not to, you should consider that by staying unmarried, the non-wage earner in your relationship will not be entitled to Social Security benefits.

As with all other unfair laws, the possibility of change lives in your congressman's office. Get involved.

2. Welfare

How will living with your partner affect your welfare benefits? Generally, a person receiv-ing AFDC benefits who begins living with her partner (who is not the child's father) can continue to receive her monthly check so long as the partner does not contribute to her support or the support of the children.

Each welfare office handles this situation differently, so it is wise to contact your local office to find out exactly what their guide-lines and requirements are so your grant will not be cut off or reduced by living with your partner.

The AFDC mother and the unrelated partner will be required to sign a statement, under penalty of perjury, declaring what amount of money, if any, he contributes to the household. The non-related partner will usually be required to pay at least his fair share of the monthly expenses. It is important to document that the non-related partner's contributions are separate, and used only for his *own* living expenses.

A non-related partner has no duty to contribute to the support of his partner's family. If the mother's grant is reduced or cut off because a non-related partner is living in the house, the mother should seek the help of the nearest Legal Aid office. Look in the white pages of your telephone book for the nearest office.

3. Other government benefits

The rules concerning medical benefits for old and poor Americans are similar to those for welfare benefits. You can have a live-in partner and still receive benefits for you and your children as long as your live-in partner does not contribute to the support of you or your children.

If you are receiving any type of government benefit and plan to begin living with your partner, you would be wise to call the local government office of the benefit program and ask what the restrictions and requirements are for live-in partners, so you can comply with their rules and not risk losing or reducing your benefits.

J. Will I inherit from my partner?

If a nonmarital partner dies without a will, the surviving partner will inherit nothing, as he or she is not considered an heir under the intestate laws—the laws that determine who inherits if a person dies without a will. A married partner would automatically inherit from a deceased spouse who dies without a will. Depending on the situation, this can leave the surviving nonmarital partner in serious financial trouble. If you are involved in a nonmarital relationship and want your partner to inherit from you, make sure you have a valid will or trust naming him or her as a beneficiary. See *Nolo's Simple Will Book* and *Make Your Own Living Trust*.

K. The tax man

Nonmarital partners are not allowed to file joint income tax returns. Depending on your income level, this may or may not be a disadvantage. Also, nonmarital partners are prohibited from claiming their partner in order to qualify as head of household. This could definitely be a disadvantage.

In addition, nonmarital partners do not have a *marital deduction*. This means that upon the death of a nonmarital partner, any inheritance left to the surviving nonmarital partner worth over $600,000 will be taxed heavily (up to 55%). $600,000 may seem like a lot of money, but with the prices of real estate in California, this could become a problem for the survivor. Contrast this with marital partners who can use their *marital deduction* to inherit any sum from their spouse, free of federal taxation.

Examples

Bill and Hillary were married for 20 years. Bill left everything he owned to Hillary—primarily a pizza franchise valued at 1 million dollars. Hillary inherits the franchise without incurring any tax liability.

Lucy and Ricky lived together for 20 years. They were not married. Ricky died and left Lucy everything in a will. Ricky owned a home, free and clear, valued at 1 million. Lucy may have to pay over $150,000 in taxes because she can't claim a *marital deduction.*

L. Can a landlord refuse to rent to us?

Landlords are prohibited under the Fair Employment Housing Act from discriminating against prospective tenants on the basis of marital status or sexual orientation.[4] An appellate court held that this law deprives landlords of free speech and religion; the issue is now before the Supreme Court.[5]

M. Domestic violence

The laws which protect against domestic violence apply to all types of nonmarital relationships.[6] Information on how to get help is found in Chapter 9.

N. If my partner is killed or injured in an accident, will I be entitled to compensation?

California has something called a wrongful death statute. It allows a marital partner to recover damages for the wrongful death of his or her spouse. However, unmarried persons are not among those authorized to bring a wrongful death action.[7]

Examples

Mickey and Minnie, married for 20 years, were at Disneyland riding Space Mountain when the car flew off the track killing Minnie. Minnie was Mickey's only means of support. Mickey would be allowed to sue Disney for the wrongful death of Minnie.

Daisy and Donald, who lived together for 20 years, were at Disneyland riding Space Mountain in the same car with Mickey and Minnie. Donald was killed and was Daisy's only means of support. Daisy cannot sue Disney under California's wrongful death laws because she and Donald were never married.

Likewise, married persons are also able to recover damages for *loss of consortium* when one spouse is injured or killed. *Consortium* encompasses companionship, love, affection, sex—all the comforts which flow from relationship. The cause of action is *strictly* confined to married partners.[8]

O. Important things to consider

If you are living together as an alternative to getting married (or because you are prohibited from getting married under California law) it is very important to have a written agreement with your partner stating which assets you intend to share, if any. The more detailed the agreement the better, and it should define all the practical and financial aspects of your life together.

Resist the "we have a loving, trusting relationship and won't end up fighting over

---

[4]Government Code §12955
[5]Smith vs. Fair Employment Housing Commn. (1994) 25 CA4th 251; SO40653. Stay tuned.
[6]Family Code §6200 et seq.
[7]Code of Civil Procedure §377.60

---

[8]*Elden vs. Sheldon* (1988) 46 C3d 267

the dishes" type of thinking. The climate of a relationship often changes unexpectedly and dramatically for many kinds of reasons. Discuss, plan and prepare for the financial and legal realities of your situation with your partner. It will prove to be a life preserver should a storm hit. Also, take the time to make a will and do some estate planning, so in the event of a partner's death, protections will be in place.

And remember, if you want your partner to make health decisions for you in the event of a medical emergency, you must prepare a durable power of attorney for health care.

In California, there is currently a push for legislation which will grant nonmarital partners many of the rights currently not available to them. Even if such legislation is eventually passed, you would still be wise to plan and prepare with your partner for unexpected events which may come to pass in the future.

We have given you a brief sketch of how the nonmarital relationship differs legally from the marital relationship. These concepts apply equally whether the relationship is hetero- or homosexual. Armed with this information, be aware that there are many good resources available to help you. We recommend Nolo's books *The Living Together Kit* and *A Legal Guide for Lesbian and Gay Couples.*

2
Getting married–Read the small print

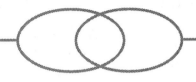

Once you start thinking about marriage, it's time to understand the rules. If you have already decided, or if you are already married, it's still not too late—it is always important to know the rules of the game you are playing. So get comfortable and pay attention; the information discussed in the chapters that follow will help save you time, trouble, money, headaches and heartache.

A. How does getting married change rights and responsibilities?

This is a loaded question and will be answered throughout the course of this book. In a very general sense, a husband and wife "contract toward each other obligations of mutual respect, fidelity, and support."[1]

Marriage is a *legal* status, from which certain rights and responsibilities automatically flow. Married couples enjoy the protections of the community property system (we will discuss this in Chapter 3) and automatic rights of inheritance. In addition, a married person becomes responsible for the well-being of their spouse. This includes providing financial support for the necessities of life. At this point we just want you to understand that upon getting married, a new set of rules apply; knowing these rules will help you to understand the legal significance of marriage.

How to find California marriage laws.
Marriage and divorce laws are state specific, which means that each state has its own set of laws. In California, much of the law governing marriage, divorce, child support, spousal support, and the like are set out in the California Family Code. In addition,

some of the rules are found in decisions that have been decided and handed down by the California appellate courts. These types of rules are collectively known as *case law.*

You can find the Family Code, which is indexed by subject, in any county law library. There is also an "annotated" version that contains excerpts from court decisions that have discussed a particular code section.

The case law is much harder to find and study. Cases are published, but not in any particular order, and cases on every subject are all mixed together. A good way to study the laws and cases on any subject you are interested in is to look them up in a legal encyclopedia. There are several, so ask your county law librarian for help. You can learn more about law libraries and legal research in Nolo's book, *Legal Research.*

B. Prenuptial agreements

Prenuptial agreements allow parties to a prospective marriage to clearly define their property rights during the marriage and in the event of divorce. You and your partner should not feel anxious about engaging in premarital "divorce planning." On the contrary, a prenuptial contract—and the negotiation and discussion which lead to its drafting—can educate both parties as to their property rights during and after marriage and illuminate some of the financial and legal implications of marriage.

The process of deciding if one or both of the partners to a prospective marriage need a prenuptial agreement should be used to encourage a feeling of working together to build a marital estate that is owned equally and fairly by both parties.

---

[1]Family Code §720

Before you can decide whether you need a prenuptial agreement, we need to give you some background on the community property system and how it will affect your property rights. Then in Chapter 5, we will further discuss prenuptial (or premarital) agreements and give you information on how to draft one.

C. How to get legally married

California defines marriage as follows:

Marriage is a personal relation arising out of a civil contract between a man and a woman, to which the consent of the parties capable of making that contract is necessary. Consent alone will not constitute marriage; it must be followed by the issuance of a license and solemnization as authorized by this division. . . .[2]

The Golden State imposes a few other requirements.

Age. California sets 18 as the minimum age for marriage. People below 18 need the consent of a parent or guardian and a Superior Court judge, who may, and probably will, require marriage counseling before giving consent.[3]

Family relationship. In California, in-laws and cousins, even first cousins, can marry. Only the following marriages are prohibited:

Marriages between parents and children, ancestors and descendants of every degree [this means grandparents and grandchildren, etc.], *and between brothers and sisters of the half as well as the whole blood, and between uncles and nieces, or aunts and nephews.* . . .[4]

Race. Unbelievable as it may sound, until 1948, it was illegal in California for whites to marry "Negroes, Mongolians, Malayans or mulattos." Statutes such as these were common in the U.S., especially in states that had rebelled against the Union to protect the institution of slavery. It was not until more than 100 years after the rebellion was crushed and black people were supposedly liberated that the U.S. Supreme Court, in the case of *Loving v. Virginia,* held that all remaining state laws regulating marriage on the basis of race were unconstitutional.[5]

Mental capacity. Insane people and the severely mentally retarded do not have the ability to enter into a contract and thus can't marry. Of course, it is very difficult to tell when a person is, or isn't, insane, and courts have held that a person who is experiencing a lucid interval between periods of insanity can enter into a marriage contract. Certainly the fact that a person has been mentally ill in the past is not a bar to marriage.

Sobriety. A person who has been drinking or is obviously under the influence of a drug will not be issued a marriage license. There are no blood alcohol tests administered; the County Clerk has discretion to decide whether a person is drunk or sober.[6]

Physical capacity. The old notion that marriage is a license to have sexual relations aimed at producing children is still with us in law as it is in religion. In theory, each party to a marriage must at least have the physical ability to have intercourse, even though the woman is past child-bearing age. A marriage where a person can't have intercourse, or can't have children, if of child-bearing age,

---

[2]Family Code §300
[3]Family Code §301
[4]Family Code §2200

---

[5]388 U.S. 1 (1967)
[6]Family Code §352

can be voided unless that fact has been completely disclosed and understood by the other person prior to marriage.

Prior marriage still valid. You can be married to only one person at a time. If either party to a marriage is married to someone else, the subsequent marriage is void. This is true *even if neither spouse knew the prior marriage was still valid.*

 Married people often file papers to get a divorce or an annulment and think this means that they can remarry. Not true—you must wait until the court issues its judgment. In California, it takes at least six months to get a divorce judgment, and often longer. Legal separations and annulments can be faster.

California recognizes any divorce or annulment legally obtained in any other state. Divorces obtained outside of the U.S. will be recognized only if the foreign court had jurisdiction to grant the divorce. This means that one of the spouses must have been a resident of the foreign country for the time necessary to be eligible to get a divorce in that country. If, at the time of the foreign divorce, both husband and wife were residents somewhere other than where the foreign divorce was granted, the foreign divorce will *not* be valid in California.[7]

If only one spouse gets the out-of-country divorce, it will probably not stand up if the other spouse challenges it. If, however, one spouse gets a divorce without the consent of the other, but both spouses act as if the divorce is valid, many courts will prevent the spouse who did not originally consent from later contesting the divorce. In some situations foreign divorces will be recognized to the extent that they end the marriage, but will not be recognized for purposes of child custody, support, visitation or property division. Obviously this is a tricky area of the law and it would be wise to see a lawyer if you have questions.

Our advice: It's very simple to obtain a divorce in California. We think it is foolish to try to save a few dollars and a few months by going out of the country. See Chapter 10 for details on how the divorce process works.

Marriage licenses. In California, there are two kinds of marriage license—a regular one and a confidential. For information on confidential marriage licenses, see Section D below. To get a regular marriage license in California, both parties must show up at the County Clerk's office and buy a license before marrying. It costs about $40. The Clerk must give all applicants a brochure published by the state Department of Health containing information about AIDS and confidential AIDS testing.[8]

---

[7]Family Code §2091

[8]Family Code §358

At the County Clerk's office, both people must state their names, ages and places of residence. The Clerk is legally prohibited from asking about race, but he or she can inquire into any of the other requirements discussed above. If either person is under 18, the Clerk must also file parental and Superior Court consent forms. The marriage license, when issued, is good for 90 days.

Ceremony and certificate of registry.
You must participate in a formal ceremony to have a marriage.

No particular form for the ceremony of marriage is required, but the parties must declare, in the presence of the person solemnizing the marriage, that they take each other as husband and wife.[9]

A marriage may be solemnized (this is the term used by the Code) by any judge or retired judge, commissioner or retired commissioner or assistant commissioner of a court of record or justice court, or by any priest, minister or rabbi (over 18) of any

[9]Family Code §420

religion. "Any religion" means just that—a minister of the Universal Life Church, or for that matter the United Evangelical Society of Polar Bear Worshippers, is just as qualified to marry you as is the Pope. The person marrying you must fill out a form called the Certificate of Registry of Marriage which will be given to you by the County Clerk when you get your marriage license. This form, along with a completed copy of the marriage license, must be filed by returning it to the Clerk within thirty days after the marriage ceremony.

Witnesses. California requires one witness to a marriage other than the spouses and the person conducting the ceremony.

D. Confidential marriages

The confidential marriage was created long ago to allow people living in "sin" to get legally married without publicly admitting (by applying for a marriage license) that they weren't married all along. For most people, living together without being married is no longer the shameful thing that it once was, but the law is still with us. The only advantage to a confidential marriage is that you get to keep it quiet—it's not a public record.

An unmarried man and an unmarried woman, who have been living together as husband and wife (no specified amount of time is required), neither of whom is under the age of 18, can marry without getting the regular license.[10]

Here's how you do it:

• Both parties appear before the County Clerk to obtain a confidential marriage license. You pay a fee, about $40, for the

[10]Family Code §500

license and other papers you'll need to complete the marriage.

- Get married in the county where the license was issued within 90 days.

- Deliver the license to the person who is marrying you—a judge, priest, rabbi or County Clerk; anyone entitled by law to solemnize marriages (see discussion of Ceremony under Section D above).

- The person who performs the marriage must return the certificate of confidential marriage to the County Clerk, typically by mail, within 30 days after the ceremony.

- The person who performs the marriage must give you a copy of the certificate and give you an application for a certified copy of your certificate.

- Fill out the application, send it to the County Clerk and receive back a certified copy of your marriage certificate.

E. Out-of-state and foreign marriages

In general, all marriages entered into outside of California that were valid under the laws of the state or country where they were made are valid in California.[11] Under this law, even a marriage entered into with the intent to circumvent California laws will be treated as good here, if it was valid where created.

There is one exception to this rule: marriages performed elsewhere that would be odious in California aren't recognized here. We don't know exactly what "odious" means, but a woman can't have more than one husband, a man can't have more than one wife and a father can't marry his daughter. Same-sex marriages fall into this category

too. Although Denmark has legalized same-sex marriages, those marriages would most likely not be recognized in California, as California limits marriage to a man and a woman marrying each other.

F. "I *thought* I was married!" The putative spouse

When a marriage is invalid because some legal requirement has not been met, an *innocent* partner may nevertheless be entitled to the protections of the community property system under what is known as the *putative marriage* doctrine.[12] However, a partner may only be declared a "putative spouse" if he or she had a good faith and objectively reasonable belief that the marriage was *legally* valid. This means you must *really* think you are married.

Example

George and Barbara got married in 1960. They had a marriage license and a small ceremony in Santa Barbara. George had been married for a few months when he was a teenager, but he never bothered to get a divorce—he just forgot about it. Barbara didn't know about this. Twenty-four years later, in 1994, George died of a heart-attack and Hillary showed up to claim George's estate. Since Barbara and George were not *legally* married—because George had never divorced Hillary—his subsequent marriage was not valid. During all those years of supposed marriage, Barbara was not legally a wife and she is in danger of losing all right to George's estate. However. *if* she can show that she is entitled to *putative spouse* status, all property acquired by George and Barbara during their *putative marriage* will be divided in the same way property is divided at the end of a valid marriage.

If you find yourself in a *putative spouse* situation, you need to contact a family law attorney in your area to ensure that your

---

[11] Family Code §308

[12] *Marriage of Vryonis* (1988) 202 CA3d 712

rights are protected. It is important to understand the rights of a lawfully married spouse, so read on; the information in this book will help you to better ascertain your rights as a *putative* spouse.

G. Common law marriages— Are they legal?

In thirteen states and the District of Columbia, if you live with a person for a certain period of time and tell people you are married, you automatically become legally married, even though you never got a marriage license or went through a ceremony. This is called a "common law" marriage.

Common law marriages are permitted in the following states:

Alabama	Montana
Colorado	Ohio
District of Columbia	Oklahoma
Georgia	Pennsylvania
Idaho	Rhode Island
Iowa	South Carolina
Kansas	Texas

In all other states, including California, there is *no such thing* as a common law marriage. Regardless of how long you live together, or what you intend, the law will *not* recognize your relationship as a common law marriage. But if you formed a valid common law marriage in a state that recognizes them and latter moved to California, you will be legally married in California.

Common law marriage is more than just living together. Even in states recognizing common law marriage, living together does not automatically result in marriage. To have a common law marriage, both parties must *intend* to be married.

Conduct showing an intent to be married usually includes using the same last name, holding yourself out to the community as married and filing joint tax returns. The length of time people live together is not in itself normally important, but may be considered insofar as it shows the intent of the parties. Once a common law marriage exists, the marriage can only be legally ended by divorce or annulment.

Whether or not you are legally married to your partner becomes an issue when you break up—do you divorce or just split up? Or when one partner dies—who inherits what? Or if a medical emergency should occur—who can authorize medical treatment? It also becomes an issue whenever you deal with government programs, such as Social Security, welfare, and so on.

If you were living with someone in one of the common law marriage states, you may wonder if you formed a legal common law marriage. To find out for sure, you will need to do some legal research into the laws of the state you came from. You could call a family law attorney from the state where you believe you formed a common law marriage, or you can save some bucks and do the research yourself. Any large county law library or law school library will have the laws from all states.

Common law marriage states have no official records of common law marriages (how could they?) but at least one, Texas, permits a couple to file a certificate of common law marriage at the County Clerk's office.

Examples

Abigail and Amos started living together in San Jose in 1957. They are still together, have never participated in a marriage ceremony and have never moved out of California. Are they married? No. They cannot create a common law marriage in California.

Wanda and Walter started living together in Colorado in 1965 with the intention of forming a common law marriage and have been living together ever since. In 1971 they moved to Los Angeles. Are they married? Yes. California will recognize the marriage as valid, because Colorado permits common law marriages and the marriage took place in Colorado before they moved to California.

If you want to stay together, but want to be sure that you are not married, it would be a good idea to type out and sign an agreement such as the following (notarization is optional):

Sample agreement: No marriage

```
Wanda Adams and Walter Bishop
agree that they have been and
plan to continue to live together
as two free independent beings
and that neither has ever in- '
tended to enter into any form of
marriage, common law or other-
wise.
```

Date	Wanda Adams

Date	Walter Bishop

If one of you believes that a marriage exists and the other doesn't and you are unable to talk the situation out, you may have to see a lawyer. But remember, anyone can get a divorce in California by simply filing a few papers and, in some situations, making an appearance down at the local courthouse, so it would only make sense to insist that a marriage exists and go through a divorce if there were substantial disagreement as to property, support, child custody, etc.

H. Can I keep my own name?

Yes—you are free to keep your own name. There is no requirement that upon marriage you must take your spouse's name. It is perfectly legal and acceptable for spouses to retain their own names after marriage. Simply continue to use your own name, and no change need occur.

I. Can we make up a new name?

In California, married people are free to keep their own names, use their spouse's name, hyphenate their names, or choose a completely new name. The key to changing a name (whether married or not) is to use the new name consistently. Changing a name by consistent use is called the usage method of name change and is perfectly legal.[13]

J. Are we required to file a joint tax return?

Under federal and California law filing a joint tax return is permissible, but not required, for married taxpayers. You and your spouse should crunch the numbers and decide how you can save the most money. Consider seeing a tax accountant for expert advice.[14]

---

[13] Code of Civil Procedure §1279.5
[14] Internal Revenue Code §6013

3
Yours, mine and ours–
The community property system

Since the beginning of human social organization, systems have existed for dealing with property acquired by a family unit. The community property system that we use in California is rooted in a property scheme devised by the nomadic Visigoths. The Visigoths brought it to Spain when they swept through southern Europe in the seventh century A.D., and it eventually found its way to the New World via the Spanish explorers.

The community property system is something of an oddity in the American legal tradition, as most of our law follows the English common law scheme. But if it is an oddity, it is a fair one. It is much more a people's system than the property tradition of England where, at least among the propertied classes, the wife was viewed as a possession of the husband and, as such, could have no equal claim to his estate.

Historically, the community property concept arose from recognition that the division of labor between husband and wife was substantially equal (usually equally backbreaking), therefore, they shared equally in the ownership of property acquired through their joint efforts. In more recent times, it was reasoned that the value of taking care of home and children was equal to the value of a salary.

California's community property system is based on the concept of partnership. Husband and wife are equal partners in life's adventure, therefore they share equally in whatever either of them earns during their marriage, even if one of them never lifts a finger or earns a dime.

Equal partners have equal rights to manage the community's financial affairs. As the closest kind of partners, spouses owe each other the highest duties of openness, honesty and responsibility in conducting those affairs.

In this chapter, we discuss how our marital property laws work, with pointers on how you can manage and protect your property rights. Dealing with debts, the negative side of property, is covered in Chapter 4.

A. What is my separate property?

1. What does "property" include?

First understand that in the legal world "property" includes everything from your toolbox to your pension. It includes debts (discussed in Chapter 4) as well as assets. It can be an idea, a song or a finger painting; the bottom line—it's most everything. So don't confine your concept of the term *property* to cars, boats, houses and furniture.

Property owned by a husband and wife who live in California generally falls into one of four basic ownership categories:

- community property
- husband's separate property
- wife's separate property

Property can also be a combination of the above; for example, the family home can easily be partly husband's separate property, partly wife's separate property, and partly community property. It all depends on exactly how the property was acquired.

One last category of property is known as *quasi-community property*. This is property acquired by a couple who lived outside of California and then moved to the state. It is treated as community property and is discussed in Section E below.

Characterization is the process of labeling an item of property as either separate or community, and will be discussed in detail below.

2. What's mine?—Separate property

Separate property is property that is owned by one spouse only. Whether a piece of property is community property or separate property is very important, especially at death or divorce.

Generally, separate property is:[1]

- All property acquired by a spouse *prior* to marriage, or acquired during marriage with premarital money;

- All property given *specifically* to one spouse by gift or inheritance;

- All rents, or profits from property acquired before marriage, or from property acquired after marriage with premarital money;

- All property acquired after the couple separates with the *intention* of divorcing.[2] But property acquired during a "trial

---

[1]Family Code §770
[2]Family Code §771

separation" with the hope of getting back together (regardless of whether the couple does in fact reunite) is still considered community property.[3]

Example

Harold and Maude met in 1978 and began living together in 1980. In 1983, they got married. Things got rough after a while, and so in 1992 they tried living apart on a trial basis. After about a year (1993), they decided they were best off permanently apart, and so they obtained a divorce. Their divorce becomes final in 1994. Here's how to *characterize* (or decide who owns) their property:

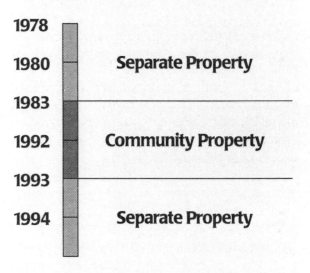

1978	
1980	**Separate Property**
1983	
1992	**Community Property**
1993	
1994	**Separate Property**

B. What is community property?

Community property is anything acquired during marriage that isn't separate property. It is owned *equally* by each spouse. Remember, under the community property system, an economic community or partnership is formed at marriage where both partners share equally in the accumulation of wealth (and debt).

Important: Spouses can determine how their property will be "classified" (separate or community). They can agree that what

---

[3]*Marriage of Marsden* (1982) 130 CA3d 426

would generally be classified as community will be the separate property of one or the other, and conversely, they can change separate property to community property by agreement. In effect, spouses can contract themselves out of part or all of the community property system. See Chapter 5.

C. "That boat we bought with my inheritance—Whose is it?" The characterization of property

Characterization is the process of determining whether an item of property is a spouse's separate property or the marriage's community property: who owns it—he, she, or we?

Generally, whether a specific item of property is community or separate depends (with a few exceptions) on when it was acquired. Let's look at the most common types of property acquired in the course of a marriage.

1. Earnings

- Wages, salaries, tips and other types of compensation earned during marriage or during any trial separation are community property.

- Wages earned prior to marriage and after separation are the earning spouse's separate property.

- It is not important when the salary is actually received; what matters is when the salary was *earned*. If earned during marriage and before separation, it is the community property of the marriage.

Example

Ozzie and Harriet got married in 1990. In 1989 Ozzie received a $5,000 bonus from his employer Burger-Heaven, payable as soon as the company had suffi-

cient cash flow. In 1991, BurgerHeaven sent Ozzie a check for $5,000. Since Ozzie earned the bonus in 1989, prior to his marriage to Harriet, the bonus would be considered his separate property even though he received it during the marriage.

2. Pensions and retirement benefits

In California, pensions and retirement benefits are a property interest—a type of deferred compensation. They are benefits paid to an employee, usually after she retires, for work done years earlier. The portion *earned* during the marriage is the community property of the marriage and the remainder is the separate property of the employee-spouse. Remember that pension plans include: state, federal and military pensions, IRAs, annuities, Keogh plans, 401(k) funds and employee stock option benefits.

So the rule is: any pension interest *earned* during marriage is community property and each spouse is entitled to a one-half share.

Military and federal pensions are treated like any other pension, unless the military retirement pay was waived in order to receive disability benefits. Military disability benefits are the separate property of the military spouse, regardless of when the right to those benefits was earned.

Spouses of marriages that lasted through ten or more years of military service gain big advantages in the enforcement of pension awards. In addition, spouses of marriages that lasted through twenty years of military service are entitled to commissary and PX benefits. If your marriage is approaching the ten- or twenty-year mark, and your spouse has served in the military during those years, don't rush into divorce until you consider what benefits will be lost.

Primary Social Security benefits are not considered community property, and thus not subject to division by California courts. Social Security is a federal program with its own rules, so contact the Social Security Administration about your rights after divorce. Be aware, however, that divorced spouses from marriages of more than ten years may be entitled to working spouse Social Security benefits when they reach retirement age.[4] So if your marriage is approaching the ten-year mark, carefully consider whether postponing your divorce will keep you eligible for benefits you will otherwise lose.

3. Disability benefits

If disability benefits are intended to replace marital earnings, they are the community property of the marriage. If they are intended to replace the postmarital earnings of the disabled spouse, they are the separate property of the disabled spouse. This is so even when the right to receive those benefits was earned during the marriage. However, if disability benefits are intended to replace a pension interest earned during the marriage, the benefits will be treated as community property.[5] (As mentioned above, this rule does not apply to military disability benefits which are always the separate property of the spouse who served.)

4. Other Employment Benefits

Benefits such as insurance, stock options, profit sharing, and the like, can be tricky because of the timing. Benefits given to an employee based on work performed during marriage—even if the benefits are received after separation—are community property.

The benefits given to an employee based on work performed before the marriage—even if the benefits are received during the marriage—are the separate property of the earner.

5. Workers' compensation

Workers' compensation benefits that are received after separation are the separate property of the injured spouse. Benefits that are received prior to separation are community property.[6]

6. Copyrights, patents, artwork and royalties

Although difficult to value, these items are community property if created, invented or generated (even if not sold) during marriage and prior to separation. Those created, invented or generated prior to marriage (even if sold during marriage) or after separation are the separate property of the creator spouse.

7. Personal injury damages

Personal injury recoveries by a husband or wife from a third party are community property when received during the marriage.[7] But when the couple divorces, the recovery is treated as the separate property of the injured spouse,[8] unless the funds were mixed with other community property, or if a judge decides that fairness requires the non-injured spouse to receive some part of the recovery.

Example

While walking across the street, Wilma was hit by a motorist who ran a stop sign. The money that Wilma

---

[4]42 U.S.C. §301 et seq. (The Social Security Act)
[5]*Marriage of Saslow* (1985) 40 C3d 848
[6]*Marriage of Fisk* (1992) 2 CA4th 1698
[7]Family Code §780
[8]Family Code §2603

recovered from the motorist was placed into a bank account she owned jointly with her husband, Herman.

- As long as Wilma and Herman are married, this money is community property. If Wilma should die, the most she could give away in her will is one-half, because Herman owns the other half.

- However, if Herman and Wilma divorce, the money will be given to Wilma, unless the couple mixed the recovery with other community property (in that case the total fund would be divided in half) or a court, after reviewing the economic needs of each party, the time elapsed since the recovery of damages, and other relevant factors, determines that justice requires Herman to receive a share. In that case, the most Herman could get is half, because at divorce, the injured spouse must be given *at least* half of any recovery.

Sound confusing? It is. In fact, one court has concluded that personal injury damages are a unique beast under California community property laws.

8. Reimbursement

Whenever a personal injury recovery, workers' compensation or disability pay is characterized (or classified) as one spouse's separate property, if community property was spent for medical or other related expenses, the community is entitled to *reimbursement.*[9]

Reimbursement is an important legal concept in the area of marriage and divorce law. It allows a spouse who has paid out money to be reimbursed by the other spouse in certain circumstances. For instance in the example above, if Wilma recovers $10,000 from the accident, and $2,000 of Wilma and Herman's community funds were paid to lawyers who handled the case, upon divorce, if Wilma is given the $10,000 recovery, the judge will also order her to reimburse Herman $1,000 for his half of the commu-

nity property which was used to pay the lawyers. Why does Wilma only have to reimburse Herman for $1,000, rather than $2,000? Since the lawyers were paid from community funds, Wilma and Herman each owned half of the money spent, so Wilma only needs reimburse Herman for his half.

Reimbursement is a way to make property division fair and equal. It usually comes into play whenever community property or one spouse's separate property has been used to benefit the other spouse alone. A classic example is when community funds are used to pay a child support obligation from a previous marriage. If separate income of the parent was available at the time but not used, then upon divorce the non-parent spouse would be entitled to reimbursement for her half of the community funds that were spent to pay her spouse's support obligation.[10]

9. Gifts and inheritances

Gifts and inheritances made specifically to one spouse or the other, no matter when given, are the separate property of that spouse. Gifts made to both spouses (like wedding gifts) are community property.[11] However, if a gift is given to one spouse in appreciation for something done by that spouse using community labor (anything done by a spouse during marriage is done with community labor), the gift will be considered the community property of the marriage.

[9] Family Code §781

[10] Family Code §915
[11] Family Code §770

Example

Kit and Kat are married. Kit is a carpenter. As a favor for his neighbor, Lula, Kit patched Lula's leaky roof. In appreciation for Kit's help, Lula gave Kit a painting he had often admired in her living room. Even though Lula specifically gave the painting to Kit, it is the community property of the marriage, owned equally by Kit and Kat. This is because Kit did the work for Lula using community labor, which then entitles Kat to half of the proceeds received from Kit's efforts.

10. Family businesses

Characterizing a family business can be tricky. Generally it works like this: businesses existing prior to marriage are separate property. The community, however, develops an interest in the business to the extent that community labor (a spouse's efforts or skills) went into running or improving the business during the marriage.

Those businesses created during marriage are community property, unless they are created with separate property. However, a community property interest will develop if any community labor is used in the creation or running of the new separate property business.

What you need to understand is that once you are married, your spouse is entitled to half of anything your talents and labor generate, whether it be a salary, an idea, or a new business.

11. Life insurance proceeds

Life insurance proceeds paid to a spouse during marriage (for example, from the death of a parent, sibling, child, or friend) are the separate property of the beneficiary spouse.[11] Where one spouse dies during marriage and a life insurance policy had been totally or partially paid for with community property, the portion of the proceeds equal to the percentage of premiums paid with community property are the community property of the marriage. Thus, the surviving spouse may claim one-half of the proceeds even if he (she) wasn't named as a beneficiary.[12]

D. How does title to property affect ownership?

Title to property is how we designate ownership. You are familiar with many types of title; for instance, the pink slip to a car. The pink slip is the car's title, it tells the world who owns it. Common types of titled assets include, houses, boats, cars, stocks and bank accounts. (Not all property has a title document; for example, items like jewelry, tools and furniture do not usually have titles.)

The following are examples of how a married person or couple normally takes title to property in California:

Separate title

- Carl Katz, a married man, as his sole and separate property.

- Kittie Katz, a married woman, as her sole and separate property.

---

[11]Family Code §770

[12]*Pattillo vs. Norris* (1976) 65 CA3d 209

Joint title

- Carl Katz and Kittie Katz, husband and wife, as community property.

- Carl Katz and Kittie Katz, as joint tenants.

- Carl Katz and Kittie Katz, as tenants in common.

1. Rules affecting title and property ownership

Several rules affect title and property ownership.

- In general, it is *presumed* that a title document accurately reflects the parties' ownership interests. To overcome the presumption that the title instrument is correct, you must show "clear and convincing" evidence of a contrary agreement or understanding.[13]

  For example, if title is in the name of one spouse alone "as separate property," you can try to show, by "clear and convincing" evidence, that it is actually community property. Conversely, if title is in the name of both you and your spouse, you may try to prove that the property is actually your separate property.

- Property acquired *during marriage* which is held in *joint title* form (tenancy in common, joint tenancy, community property or as "husband and wife") is presumed to be community property at divorce, unless a spouse shows in a deed, written agreement or other document that the asset is intended to be the separate property of one spouse.[14]

- If a spouse changes title to property from separate property to any joint-title form during the marriage, the property is con-

sidered to have been "acquired" by the couple during marriage and thus presumed to be community property. The original owner spouse, however, may be entitled to *reimbursement* (see discussion of reimbursement above) for the separate property contribution, unless he or she expressly waived (gave up) that right in writing.[15] The following agreement can be used to make such a waiver.

Sample waiver agreement

```
I, [your name], hereby make a
gift to the community of [you and
your spouse's names], my [item]
and waive all rights to be reim-
bursed for my separate property
contribution should we later
divorce.
```

Date   Signature

2. Taking title to a house

The largest purchase a couple can make is a house. Thus, we will spend a few moments going over aspects of the purchase process as they relate to your title options.

When buying a house, you must go through a formal transfer procedure, called "escrow." Escrow is supervised by an escrow agent, who computes different charges and pays miscellaneous expenses. The escrow agent also makes sure that the buyers deposit the money into an account and the sellers deliver a new deed to the house, naming the buyer as the new owner. In Northern California, escrow is normally handled by a title insurance company; in Southern California, by an escrow company.

---

[13]Evidence Code §662; *Marriage of Weaver* (1990) 224 CA3d 478
[14]Family Code §2581

[15]Family Code §2640; *Marriage of Fabian* (1986) 41 C3d 440

During escrow, you'll have to decide how to take title. This subject, along with sample documents, is covered in *The Deeds Book,* by Mary Randolph, and *How to Buy a House in California,* by Warner, Serkes and Devine, both published by Nolo Press.

One spouse's name only. If one spouse will own the house separately, title should be taken in that name alone, and the couple should sign and record, with the deed, an agreement declaring their intention that one spouse owns the house as his or her separate property. Otherwise, if the couple divorces and disagrees about ownership, a court will characterize the property as community property or separate property depending on what funds (community or separate) paid for the mortgage, insurance, improvements and taxes, rather than by whose name is on the deed. Because most couples mix and spend community and separate funds without regard to type, what property was used to make payments won't always be clear. The point to get here is that if you intend the house to be separate property, *make sure that intention is in writing.*

Joint tenancy. Joint tenancy means that the couple (joint tenants) equally share property ownership and each has the right to use the entire property. If one joint tenant dies, the survivor *automatically* inherits the deceased person's share without a probate hearing (a probate hearing is the procedure for settling a deceased person's estate). When a joint tenant dies, the property passes immediately and directly to the surviving joint tenant, even if there is a will to the contrary. If a joint tenant sells her portion to a third party or unilaterally (without consent of the other joint tenant) changes her own interest to a tenant in common, the joint tenancy ends.

Sometimes, a spouse puts a separate property house into joint tenancy with the other spouse—either as a gift to the spouse, or more usually (and more disturbing) at the request of a lending institution when the house is refinanced. Unless the spouses sign an agreement stating that the property is to remain the separate property of the spouse who originally owned it, it will be considered community property if they divorce. Again, make sure that your intentions are in writing, signed by both you and your spouse.

See Chapter 5 for sample agreements to carry out your property ownership intentions.

Tenancy in common. "Tenancy in common" means that each spouse owns separately and is entitled to equal use of the property, but they need not own equal shares. Also, if one owner dies, the other does not take her share unless this has been specified in the deceased person's will or other estate planning document. Tenancy in common is normally more appropriate for business partners than for spouses. Spouses who don't want an automatic right of survivorship as in "joint tenancy" should consider the community property alternative discussed below.

Couples who separate and want to continue to own a house together or couples who contribute separate property of the husband and separate property of the wife to a house and want to keep ownership shares clear will find that tenancy in common makes sense. See Chapter 5 for a sample agreement.

Community property. Community property ownership offers two advantages:

• Avoiding formal probate when a spouse dies; and

• Easy qualification for a federal income tax break.

When one spouse dies, property held as community property goes directly to the surviving spouse without formal probate, unless the deceased spouse left her one-half community interest to someone other than her spouse. A surviving spouse who inherits community property needs only to file a simple affidavit (available from a title insurance company) with the probate court. This can be done without a lawyer; the survivor avoids lengthy delays in transferring the property (and title), and costly probate fees. See Nolo's book, *How to Probate an Estate*.

When title is held in community property, a surviving spouse who inherits the property may have a tax advantage that she would not have for property held in tenancy in common or joint tenancy. The tax advantage hinges on the *tax basis* of the asset.

A tax basis is basically the dollar amount you spend for an asset, plus the cost of any capital improvements (swimming pool, new kitchen etc.) So if you buy a house for $100,000, the tax basis on that home is $100,000. Why do you care about the tax basis? You care because the IRS cares—the tax basis of an asset is used to determine if you lost or made money when and if you sell the asset. If you made money, the IRS wants to collect capital gain taxes from you. For instance, the house you buy in 1990 for $100,000, has a $100,000 tax basis. If you sell the house in 1992 for $150,000, you will have a $50,000 taxable capital gain. (The taxable gain is the difference between the selling price and the original tax basis.)

Here's how holding title in community property can be a big advantage. On the death of one spouse the surviving spouse receives a "stepped-up" tax basis on the entire property. This means that the surviving spouse can use the fair market value of the house at the time of her spouse's death as a tax basis (known as a "stepped-up" basis), should she decide to sell. If the title was not held in community property, only the deceased's spouses share of the asset would receive a "stepped-up" basis. Did we lose you? Here's an example to illustrate the concept:

Example

In 1979, John and Yoko, a married couple, buy a house for $100,000 and take title as tenants in common, each owning a half interest. In 1984 John is killed. John left Yoko his share of the house in his will. After a long and costly probate, Yoko finally gets title to the house in her name. Yoko decides to sell the house and return to Japan. She sells it for $200,000. (At the time of John's death, the house was also worth $200,000.) Yoko has a tax basis of $150,000; when she inherited John's half of the house, she also received a "stepped-up" tax basis for his half equal to the fair market value of the house (at John's death, the house was worth $200,000; since he owned half, the "stepped-up" tax basis is $100,000 for his share; Yoko must keep her original basis, half of the value of the house when they purchased it or $50,000—thus her total basis is $150,000). Yoko will have to pay tax on the difference between her total tax basis for the house and what she sold it for, or $50,000 ($200,000 – $150,000).

This scenario could have been avoided if John and Yoko had taken title in community property. For tax purposes, a surviving spouse's one-half share of community property is treated in the same way as the property the surviving spouse inherits from the deceased spouse (meaning the surviving spouse's share of community property will also receive a "stepped-up" basis). Thus all community property (the surviving and decedent spouse's shares) receive a new stepped-up basis equal to the fair market value of the home at the time of the deceased spouse's death. Yoko would not have a $50,000 tax liability (since she would have a $200,000 basis) if she and John had taken title in community property.

So pay attention to how you take title to an asset and seek expert help if you don't fully understand the various options and their implications.

E. What if we just moved to California?

The preceding discussion about community property in California assumes that you and your spouse have lived in California for the duration of your marriage. But what if you and your spouse acquired property while living in another state, especially a state that doesn't follow community property rules, and then moved to California?

As a general rule, *all* real or personal property that *would* have been community property had you been living in California when the items or their source were acquired is called "quasi-community" property and is treated the same as community property. However, for probate purposes, quasi-community property does not include real property located in another state. [16]

Example

Burt deposited $10,000 of income he earned during marriage when he and Loni lived in Florida. They move to California and deposit the $10,000 in the bank. The money is considered quasi-community property, as it would have been community property had Burt and Loni been living in California when Burt earned it.

At divorce, quasi-community property is divided the same way community property is split. As a practical matter, however, California courts may have trouble asserting authority over quasi-community property still outside the state.

F. When separate and community property get mixed—How to keep separate property separate

If you are in a situation where you have separate property and wish to keep it your separate property after marriage, there is one simple rule: *Do not mix your separate property with the community property of the marriage.*

This means that if you have $10,000 in a savings account prior to marriage, and wish to keep that money your separate property after you are married, keep the money in a separate account, in your name only, and don't use that account for any community funds. Or, if you use that $10,000 to buy a house with your spouse, and you want to keep the $10,000 interest separate, draw up a simple agreement reflecting your intentions (see Chapter 5).

Again, you and your spouse should not feel like you are "planning for divorce" or being distrustful by being responsible and managing your assets clearly. Just as the person who buys health insurance is not planning for sickness, neither are partners to a marriage who plan legally and financially for the future planning for a divorce. In the sweetest of love stories, divorce and death are realities. Discussing these types of issues should be seen as promoting your relationship, your love relationship. Should disaster strike, whether it be divorce or death, careful, thoughtful planning will be priceless—we

---

[16]Family Code §125; Probate Code §66.

can't stress enough the importance of this point.

1. Changing title to property

As we discussed above, determining how title to property is held is a beginning step in determining the ownership and status of property. It is not, however, conclusive. Therefore, if you want to make a gift to your spouse or change the title to your separate property, you must take the following two steps to ensure that the change is valid:

- If it is an asset with a title document, change the way title is described on the deed or motor vehicle registration, and record the deed with the county recorder's office (for real property); and

- Make a separate written agreement reflecting the change. Drafting this agreement will eliminate the possibility of the ownership being determined by who paid for the property.[17] See Chapter 5 for sample agreements to be used when changing the title of property.

A *transmutation* is an agreement between spouses to change the character or ownership of an asset. Prior to 1985, a transmutation could be oral, written or inferred from the conduct of the parties. After 1985, however, a transmutation must be in writing to be enforceable. (The writing requirement does not apply to personal gifts between spouses, such as clothing or jewelry.)

Example

Charles and Di wed in 1988. Charles owns a substantial amount of property which he acquired prior to marriage, thus it is his separate property. Charles

---

[17]Family Code §852; Gifts of clothing or jewelry for personal use need no written agreement, nor do gifts made before January 1, 1985. See *Estate of Blair* (1988) 199 CA3d 161

decides that he wants one of his small country estates to be community property, and thus half-owned by Di. He changes the title document to reflect his gift to Di and records it in the county recorder's office. In addition he signs an agreement which states his intention. Charles has effectively *"transmuted"* his separate property to community property.

2. Combining Property

Spouses frequently combine or "commingle" separate property and community property without thinking through how this changes the character of the property. If there is no agreement showing the intent of the spouses, problems arise at divorce.

Combining usually takes two forms— separate property used to make permanent improvements on something owned by the community (or vice versa) or community and separate property (or wife's separate and husband's separate property) combined to purchase one item. Chapter 5 contains sample agreements to be used when combining property.

Example

Two years ago Bill got married. Right before the ceremony, he borrowed $10,000 from his mother, signing a note which his future wife, Elaine, didn't sign because she wasn't around. The couple deposited the money, which was to buy land, into a joint bank account. They made many deposits and withdrawals on that account, so the balance fluctuated widely. Eventually, they bought land for $8,000 and put it in both names. Then Elaine filed for divorce and claimed that the $2,000 left in the bank, as well as the land, was community property, but that the $10,000 owed Bill's mother was his separate debt. Bill thinks this is unfair and wants to know if he has a leg to stand on.

Bill may be able to prove that the debt is a community debt or that the land is his separate property. However, Bill would be in a far better legal position if either Elaine had signed the original note, or if Elaine and Bill had signed an agreement recognizing that the land was Bill's separate property. Need we say more about the value of doing business in a businesslike way?

G. Management of community property

A spouse who manages community property on behalf of the marriage owes a duty of the "highest degree of good-faith" or what is called a *fiduciary duty* to the other spouse and may be sued during the marriage (or as part of a divorce) for the breach of this duty.[18] The duty requires each spouse to do their utmost to preserve the assets of the community. For example, Janis and Tom keep a savings account of community property in Janis's name for the benefit of the community. If Janis uses this money to travel around the world with her lover while Tom believed the money was being saved for a house, upon divorce Tom could sue Janis for breach of her fiduciary duty of "highest degree of good-faith" owed Tom.

A spouse who manages a community property business may generally act without the other spouse's consent. However, if the managing spouse intends to sell or give away all or most of the property of the business, he must first receive the non-managing spouse's written consent. For example, a spouse running a couple's business may make day-to-day business decisions, including buying goods for the store, entering into leases, hiring and firing employees and deciding what to sell, without the other's consent.[19] However, the spouse-manager cannot sell the business unless the non-managing spouse consents in writing. (All decisions made by the managing spouse *must* be designed to preserve the assets of the community.)

The managing spouse also encounters limitations if she tries to give away community property. (See Section H below.)

Don't deliberately damage community property. If you're angry at your spouse, don't take it out on the community property. A wife who threw a bottle at the couple's Mercedes was convicted of vandalism, which is defined as maliciously damaging property not your own. The wife argued that she couldn't be guilty of vandalizing her own property. The court disagreed, emphasizing that because each spouse owns half of the community property, criminal laws protect each owner from "unilateral nonconsensual damage or destruction by the other."[20]

The legislation which demands that each spouse act with the "highest degree of good-faith" toward each other is broad and has teeth which can bite. So if you are thinking of cheating your spouse or hiding assets, or in some other way interfering with your spouse's property rights, we have only this advice—**DON'T**.

H. Can I sell or give community property away?

Each spouse may give away his or her own separate property without the other's consent. Of course, neither spouse can give away the other's separate property without consent. The rules are different when community property is involved.

---

[18]Family Code §1100, 1101 & 1102
[19]Family Code §1100

[20]*People vs. Kahanic* (1987) 196 CA3d 461

1. Giving away community property

Neither spouse can legally make a gift of any community property without the consent of the other. A gift is any transfer of property without the giver getting something of roughly equivalent value in exchange. For instance, a transfer of title to a house in exchange for $1,000 would most likely be considered a gift. Written consent is required for any gift of community property furniture, clothing and real property.

2. Selling community personal property

Either spouse can sell personal community property, except home furnishings and clothing, without the written consent of the other spouse.

If one spouse gives away or sells furniture or clothing without the consent of the other, the non-consenting spouse can sue to set aside the transfer. The spouse must sue within three years of the gift or sale of personal community property (furniture or clothing).

3. Selling community real property

Neither spouse can sell, mortgage, lease for more than a year, or otherwise transfer any real community property without the written consent of the other spouse. If one spouse gives away, sells or otherwise transfers any real property, the non-consenting spouse must sue within three years from when the new deed is recorded.

A gift or sale of community property by one spouse can cause problems, especially if the couple later divorces. When people are stressed and upset, they often escalate minor disagreements into something approaching war. The best way to avoid confusion is to make a short agreement when either spouse sells or gives away an item of value and put it in the file where you keep the important papers. You may think that keeping records is too much trouble and that it's easier to trust your spouse. In marriage, as in business, trust is the basic building block of a good relationship. But trust can erode fast if people don't take steps to protect it.

4
Debts: Who owes what?

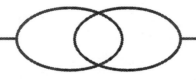

While most couples accumulate assets and debts during marriage, others just rack up debts—sometimes big ones. It is important to know which debts you are responsible for and to what extent you are liable for your spouse's debts. Remember, when you marry, you become legally and financially connected to your partner. So *don't skip this chapter!*

A debt is an obligation to pay someone money. It may be a large obligation, such as a home mortgage or monthly rent, or a small obligation, like a monthly newspaper bill. If you don't pay, you usually suffer negative consequences. At the *serious trouble* end of the scale, if you don't pay your mortgage or rent, your house may be foreclosed or you may be evicted. At the *minor inconvenience* end, if you don't pay your *People* magazine subscription, it will be canceled and you'll have to pick one up each week at the news stand.

In this chapter you will find an overview of how liability for debts is determined. The discussion covers both debts incurred by a married couple and debts incurred by one spouse before marriage.

A. Am I responsible for my spouse's premarital debts?

Generally, a spouse is not liable for the separate debts their partner incurred before marriage.[1] This means that your separate property cannot be taken in order to pay a credit card bill your spouse ran up before you were married.

However, even though your separate property can't be taken, *all* of the *community property*, including *your* half, can be attached by a creditor to pay your spouse's premarital debts. You can exempt your wages from this rule *if* you deposit them in a separate account, and do not mix or *commingle* them with any other community property. This means your spouse must have *no* access to the separate account.[2]

Because it is possible for a creditor to reach your half of the community property to pay your spouse's premarital debts, this means that if you or your spouse comes into the marriage with significant debt, you should discuss setting up a separate account for the non-debtor spouse's community property wages. You should write an agreement that states your intention to keep his or her earnings separate. (See Chapter 5 for a sample agreement.)

Example

When Marie and Pierre married, Marie had student loan debts of $10,000. She had defaulted on four payments of $150 each prior to marriage, and has continued to default during marriage. The bank can go after Marie's separate property, and then Marie and Pierre's community property, to satisfy her student loan debts.

Before we go on to explain who owes what for debts incurred during the marriage, we want to take a side trip into secured and unsecured debts.

B. Secured and unsecured debts

1. Secured Debts

Secured debts are linked to specific items of property, called "collateral." The collateral guarantees payment of the debt—if you

---

[1] Family Code §913

[2] Family Code §§911, 915; *Marriage of Williams* (1989) 213 CA3d 1239

don't pay, the creditor can take the property. If you've ever had a car repossessed when you failed to pay a loan, you already know a lot about how secured debts work. However, the creditor does not have to take back the collateral and can try other methods to collect the money you owe. For example, if you still owe $7,500 on your new car loan, but recently wrecked the car, the creditor won't repossess it—creditors want dollars, not dents. Even if they do repossess, they can sell the property for a song and still come after you for the balance due.

When you take out a secured loan, you always sign a *security agreement* with the creditor. This agreement specifies precisely what property (collateral) can be taken by the creditor if you default on the loan. The security agreement also creates a *lien*—the creditor's legal right to take possession of the collateral in the event you don't pay. Security agreements are of two kinds:

a. Purchase money. Here you pledge the property you are in the act of buying—usually motor vehicles, furniture, large appliances or electronics equipment—as the collateral. This is the most common type of security agreement. Here are some common examples of purchase money security agreements:

- Mortgages (deeds of trust)—loans to buy or refinance a house or other real estate. The house or other real estate is collateral for the loan. If you fail to pay, the lender can foreclose.

- Loans for cars, boats, tractors, motorcycles, RVs—the vehicle is the collateral.

- Store charges with a security agreement—for example, when you buy furniture or a major appliance, many department or appliance stores require you to sign a security agreement in which you agree that the item purchased is collateral for your repayment. Keep in mind that only a few store charges come with security agreements. Most store purchases are unsecured.

b. Nonpurchase money. Here you borrow a sum of money and pledge some other piece of property you already own as security. Some common examples of nonpurchase money security agreements include:

- Home equity loans (also called second mortgages) from banks or finance companies—such as loans to make improvements on your house. The house or other real estate is collateral for the loan. If you fail to pay, the lender can foreclose.

- Personal loans from finance companies—often your valuable personal property, such as a paid-off motor vehicle, is pledged as collateral.

2. Unsecured Debts

With unsecured debts there is no collateral. For example, you charge a suit on a store credit card but don't sign a security agreement specifying that the suit is collateral for your repayment. With no collateral, the creditor has nothing to take if you don't pay. This leaves the creditor only one option if she wants to be paid: to sue you, get a judgment for the money you owe and try to collect it. To try to collect, she can go after your wages, bank account or other property that can be taken to satisfy money judgments.

Let us not forget the damage that can be done to a credit report by a creditor who has not been paid. Negative reports to credit agencies can ruin your credit for years to come.

Most debts people incur are unsecured. Some of the more common ones are:

- Accountants' and lawyers' bills

- Alimony and child support

- Church or synagogue dues

- Credit and charge card cash advances

- Credit and charge card purchases (such as Visa, MasterCard, American Express and Discover)

- Gasoline and most department store charges

- Health club dues

- Loans from friends or relatives

- Medical bills

- Rent

- Student loans

- Union dues

- Utility bills

C. "Our" new car: Debts and marriage

As a general rule, both spouses are responsible for debts incurred by either or both spouses during marriage *unless* the debt in no way benefits the community. This rule follows the theme that once a couple is married, they become marital partners and thus share assets *and debts* equally. Here are the rules:

- The *separate property* of one spouse usually cannot be taken by a creditor to pay the separate debts of the other spouse. Separate property of one spouse can be taken to pay *joint* debts, and separate property of one spouse is always available to pay his or her own separate debts.

There is an exception: the separate property of a spouse can be taken to pay separate debts of the other incurred during marriage *if* the debt is for the "necessaries of life" (e.g., food, clothing, medical care) and there is no separate property of the debtor spouse or community property available to pay for it.[3]

Example

Oliver and Sylvia are both in their 70s. Sylvia owns the home they live in as her separate property. Oliver's faculties have been diminishing lately and Sylvia is concerned that if Oliver gets into a car accident, her house could be sold to pay his debts. If Oliver injures another person or person's property, Sylvia's property is safe from Oliver's creditors, as those debts would not be for Oliver's "necessaries." If Oliver needs medical treatment, however, Sylvia's separate property would be liable, as medical care for Oliver is a "necessary of life."

- Spouses are generally not liable for the separate debts their mate incurred after *separation* (unless the debt was incurred for the "necessaries of life").[4]

- Both spouses are generally liable for all debts incurred during marriage unless the creditor was clearly looking to only one spouse for credit. "During marriage" does not include the time between separation and divorce.[5] There are four exceptions to this rule:

1. If a creditor relied on the separate property of one spouse alone as collateral, the debt is not a community debt, and only the spouse to whom the creditor looked for repayment is responsible for the debt. For example, if a spouse bought a kayak putting financial information only about himself on the loan application—such as a bank account

---

[3]Family Code §914
[4]Family Code §910
[5]Family Code §910

with funds containing money owned before marriage—his spouse would not be liable to pay for the kayak if he defaults on the loan.

2. For community property to be used to pay a debt, the debt must not promote the breakdown of the marriage. If the debt is of no benefit to the community, the spouse who benefits by the debt will be solely responsible for its repayment.[6] For example, if two weeks before separating, one spouse treats her lover to a trip to Hawaii (while claiming to be on a business trip), the spouse who stayed home can argue that the Hawaii trip is the other spouse's separate debt. When we say "no benefit to the community," we mean no benefit. A bill for books on a subject only one spouse is interested in is a community debt because it enhances that spouse, which in turn enhances the community. The same generally can't be said about the Hawaii trip.

3. If one spouse is held liable for some harm coming to the other, the community property may not be liable. (See a lawyer if this applies to you.)

4. Debts incurred between separation and divorce for necessaries (food, housing, clothing and health care) for a spouse or children are considered joint debts, unless there is a child support order stating who must pay. A creditor may obtain payment from either spouse. If the wife pays, but the husband incurred the debt, the wife will not be entitled to reimbursement.

Example

George and Fran separated in October and planned to divorce. In December, George was in a car accident, and was billed $250 for fixing the car and $100 toward his medical costs. In March, when George and Fran drafted their divorce agreement, George requested that Fran contribute toward the bills. Fran refused, so they brought the question before a judge. The judge ordered George to pay the full car bill, but ordered Fran to help with the medical costs (a "necessary" of life).

D. If I co-sign my spouse's loan, can they get my separate property?

Yes! Co-signing any type of loan agreement with your spouse is the quickest way to make your separate property liable for community debts. If one spouse takes out a loan, or otherwise obtains credit, and the other spouse signs the security agreement or loan, this means that in addition to the couple's community property, the separate property of *both* spouses is liable for the debt. So don't just sign a credit agreement without thinking. If a wife puts her name on her husband's credit card account, for example, her separate property is liable for any debts he may run up. In other words, money she earned prior to marriage and money she inherits during marriage is liable should he charge $1,500 on his credit card before buying a one-way ticket to Costa Rica.

E. Tax Debts

Taxes, especially federal income taxes, can raise special problems. Frequently, one spouse enters the marriage owing taxes, and the other spouse is concerned that she may be required to foot the bill. The rule is that the spouse who owes the taxes is liable for the debt. This means all of her separate property can be taken to satisfy the IRS debt. It also means that *all* community property, including the non-debtor spouse's wages, can be taken if they are deposited in a

---

[6]Family Code §2625

joint account. If you or your spouse owe a large sum in back taxes, set up a separate account for the non-debtor spouse and explore the option of a premarital or marital agreement, setting forth your agreement to keep your property separate. (See Chapter 5.)

If you owe back taxes for a year you were married and filed jointly, even if the bill comes after your divorce is final, both spouses are liable. You *may* be able to reduce or minimize your own liability (this is called the "innocent spouse" rule) if:

- The bill is for unreported income in excess of 25% of the amount originally reported, you didn't know or had no reason to know of the under-reporting, and you did not significantly benefit from the omitted income; or

- The bill is for omitted income or an illegal deduction, you didn't know or had no reason to know that there was an understatement of your tax liability, and it would be unfair to hold you liable for the taxes owed.

F. "We can't pay our bills"—bankruptcy

For couples overwhelmed by their debt burden, declaring bankruptcy may be an option. In most cases, bankruptcy lets you erase your debts in exchange for giving up "non-exempt" property. (Certain items of property, such as household goods and furniture, clothing, certain equity in a home, certain equity in a car and several other items are exempt. You get to keep exempt property when you file for bankruptcy.) Married couples can file for bankruptcy jointly, or one spouse can file as an individual.

Before deciding to file, you *must* understand how bankruptcy works and how it will affect your particular situation. Bankruptcy is not for everyone—make sure you look before you leap! See Nolo's books *How to File for Bankruptcy* and *Chapter 13 Bankruptcy*.

If a married couple files for bankruptcy together, they can eliminate all the separate debts of the husband, separate debts of the wife and all jointly incurred marital debts.[7] If only one spouse files, that spouse can eliminate his or her separate debts, as well as both spouses' obligation to pay the *community* debts. This means that only one spouse needs to file a bankruptcy petition in order for both spouses to receive the benefit of a discharge of community debts.[8] However, the non-filing spouse, remains responsible for paying any of his or her own separate debts.

There are additional factors which should be considered before determining whether one

---

[7]Some debts cannot be erased (discharged) in bankruptcy. The most common ones are recent taxes, student loans first payable within the past seven years, child support, spousal support and debts incurred by a fraudulent act on your part.

[8]11 U.S.C. §§523(a), 524(a)(3)

or both spouses should file for bankruptcy; we suggest you thoroughly explore your options. Nolo's *How To File For Bankruptcy* is a good information source, or you may want to seek expert help from a bankruptcy attorney.

It is important to understand that dividing debts at divorce does not affect your original relationship with your creditors. Just because Russ agreed to pay back the community debt to Sears doesn't mean that Sears cannot go after his ex-wife Mary for the payments, if Russ fails to pay. Creditors are not interested in your agreement with your ex-spouse—they are only interested in getting their money.

How does a bankruptcy affect your marital settlement agreement or dissolution judgment? We need to answer this question in two parts. Let's look at the clear-cut part first.

Support obligations made pursuant to a court order or judgment are not dischargeable in bankruptcy.[9] This includes debts that are assumed as a substitute for paying support—or in exchange for paying lower support.

Marital debts which are generally considered a substitute for support and not dischargeable include those that:

- Are paid to an ex-spouse who maintains the primary home of the children, while there is a serious imbalance of incomes;

- Terminate on the death or remarriage of the recipient;

- Depend on the future income of either spouse;

- Are paid in installments over a substantial period of time—usually several years.

Back child support or alimony may *only* be discharged in the following situations:

Support was owed under a state's general support law, rather than a court order. If your support debt arose under a general state law to support a child or spouse and no court actually ordered the support, the debt is dischargeable. This is true even if the creditor is the welfare department, which wants you to reimburse it for benefits paid before a court issued a child support order.

Support was owed under an agreement between unmarried persons. If an unmarried couple enters into an agreement that includes support, the obligation can be discharged in bankruptcy unless one person won a lawsuit against the other and obtained a court judgment for the support.

Support was owed someone other than a spouse, ex-spouse or child. If an ex-spouse or child gave ("assigned," in legal terms) the right to receive the support to someone else—such as a creditor with a judgment against that person—the debt is dischargeable, unless it is owed to the welfare department. When it is owed to the welfare department, the debt is treated the same as when it is owed to the ex-spouse or child—that is, it cannot be discharged in bankruptcy.

The second part of the answer is more complicated. Recent legislation[10] enacted by Congress provides that bankruptcy will not free a debtor spouse from an obligation that relates to marital property rights[11] (such as the division of community debts in a divorce action). However, there are two big exceptions in this new law. The debts *can* be discharged if:

---

[9]11 U.S.C. §523(a)(5)

[10]Applies to bankruptcy actions commenced on or after 10/22/94.
[11]11 U.S.C. §523 (a)

1. The debtor is unable to pay the debt from income or property that is not reasonably necessary to support the debtor or his or her dependents; or if applicable, to continue the debtor's business; or

2. If the discharge would result in a benefit to the debtor that outweighs the resulting detriment to a spouse, former spouse, or child of the debtor.

What do these exceptions really mean? We don't know—but it is certain there will be plenty of litigation in finding out.

Regardless of whether your ex-spouse is allowed to discharge non-support type marital debt in a bankruptcy proceeding, you are still responsible to the creditors for that debt (even though it was assigned to your ex-spouse in the divorce), and if he or she doesn't pay, the creditor may come after you for payment. If the bankruptcy court refuses to allow your ex to discharge the debt, and you pay it, then you would have to sue your ex to get your money back. (Another option, of course, would be for you to file bank-ruptcy as well.)

Example

Russ and Mary divorce in 1994. In the divorce Russ is ordered to pay $5,000 marital debt owed to Visa. Russ files for bankruptcy in January 1995. Meanwhile, Russ hasn't made a payment to Visa in several months. The bankruptcy court refuses to allow Russ to discharge the marital debt. Mary who was being hounded by Visa, paid the bill. Mary must now bring an action against Russ to get her money back

Here's another look at how one spouse can potentially be burned by a bankrupt ex-spouse. Assume that Kathleen and Paul divorce. Kathleen receives a larger share of the community property, so she gives Paul a promissory note for $35,000, to even up the property division. A year later, Kathleen is dead broke and can't pay Paul, so she files for bankruptcy and asks the court to erase her obligation to make good on the note to Paul. If the bankruptcy court allows the discharge, Paul falls $35,000 short in getting his share of the marital property. And even if the bankruptcy court won't allow her to discharge the debt, she is still dead broke and can't pay Paul.

Paul could have better protected himself by having the promissory note *secured* (see Section B above) by the house—assuming Kathleen keeps the house. This kind of secured note would allow him to force the sale of the house if she doesn't pay. Also, a secured promissory note can't be erased by bankruptcy if the security interest (the note securing the house) is created at the same time the house is transferred from both spouses to the spouse keeping it after the marriage.[12] This is a very tricky area of law; if it applies to you, see a bankruptcy lawyer.

---

[12] *Farrey vs. Sanderfoot* (1991) 111 S.Ct. 1825

Bankruptcy isn't for everyone. It stays on your credit record for ten years, although in some cases you are able to rebuild your credit and obtain credit in two or three years after filing. Nonetheless, be sure you understand that bankruptcy is always a possibility (unless you filed within the previous six years) for you and your spouse. If you're overwhelmed by your debt burden, don't immediately count it out. If your spouse assumes a large share of the community debt or owes you a large sum to even up the property division, be on the lookout for any bankruptcy filing, especially if your ex starts to complain loudly about being broke.

Make sure your divorce agreement doesn't leave you vulnerable. Promissory notes, especially unsecured notes (notes that don't give you a lien on property), *can* be wiped out in bankruptcy.[13] You may have a little more protection with secured notes, but don't count on it.[14] You might be able to protect yourself by specifying in the settlement agreement that the promissory note or other payments are made in lieu of alimony.

When negotiating a divorce settlement or marital settlement agreement, keep in mind that even though an ex-spouse is ordered to pay a debt, if he or she has no money, they won't pay and you may be forced to. Now more than ever it is essential for spouses with overwhelming marital debt to get sound legal advice regarding the best way to handle the situation. If you want to file for bankruptcy, be sure you know what's involved, and whether or not it is a good choice for your particular circumstances.

---

[13] 11 U.S.C. §523 (a)(5)

[14] A secured promissory note can't be erased by bankruptcy *if* the security interest (the note secured by the property) is created at the same time the house is transferred from the two spouses to the spouse keeping the house after marriage. If your spouse has a separate property house and gives you a promissory note secured by that house—or if you transfer title in your community property house from the two of you to your spouse a month, week or even a day before you get the promissory note secured by the house—your ex-spouse will probably be able to wipe out the note in bankruptcy.

5
Marriage and pre-marriage contracts

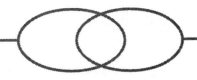

An essential aspect of marriage still escapes many prospective partners: marriage, at its core, is a *contract*. Indeed, California law defines marriage as a "civil contract."[1]

When you enter into the marriage contract by purchasing a license and saying "I do," you are subscribing to a whole system of rights and responsibilities. Unlike most other contracts, however, you never get the chance to read the terms or the fine print because the provisions are not handed to you in writing. Some of the rights and obligations of the marriage contract are contained in the massive volumes containing California laws, but many appear only in the decisions of lawsuits.

In few other legal areas are contracting parties so much in the dark. Indeed, there is usually more bargaining power and more options surrounding a contract made with a fast-talking door-to-door salesperson than when it comes to getting married. If all men and women were required to read the "marriage contract" and consider the rights and obligations contained in it prior to getting married, it would be interesting to see how many would still be willing to say "I do" with so little negotiation and planning.

Now that you have some understanding of how the community property system works and how your rights and responsibilities change when you get married, it's time to show you how to modify the community property contract to better serve the needs of you and your partner.

A. Prenuptial (pre-marriage) agreements

There was a time when prenuptial agreements were used primarily by wealthy men and women who feared their prospective mates were marrying them for the big house and the big car. Now, however, more and more couples are using premarital agreements to tailor their property rights to fit their particular circumstances and beliefs, rather than waiting until divorce to have their property rights determined by ever-changing rules established by an often non-responsive, unenlightened legislature. Essentially a premarital agreement allows parties to a marriage to modify or even contract out of the California community property system and implement, instead, an agreement that better suits their needs.

Premarital agreements can be used effectively to set forth in advance of death or a divorce a determination of property rights that is felt to be fair and reasonable to both spouses. As with most things, the time to plan for an event is long before it happens.

A pre-marriage contract that changes property ownership and division won't meet too much opposition in the courthouse.[2] Changing other areas of the marital relationship, however, such as support or child custody, will not be met with equal favors and, in fact, will not be enforced by a court unless the judge who examines the agreement agrees that its provisions are fair.

Remember, unless you and your spouse set out an agreement specifying how you'll own your property, you're stuck with the way the community property laws of California

---

[1] Family Code §300

[2] *Marriage of Grinius* (1985) 166 CA3d 1179

dictate ownership (the community property system is explained in Chapter 3).

There are many reasons why a couple might contemplate a premarital agreement. Most often, a couple will simply want to run their own financial affairs and not be subject to California's community property rules. For example:

- A wife who expects large earnings or an interest in a business or professional practice might want the assurance that the money will remain her separate property after the marriage.

- A husband who has large holdings of property may want to provide that his property and its proceeds will remain separate property after marriage regardless of the amount of community time and effort expended in its management.

- Spouses who have each been through a nasty divorce where lots of property had been mixed together and was laboriously and expensively separated may want a contract to ensure that this will never happen again.

- A husband or a wife might want to convert part or all of his or her separate property into community property.

- A wealthy, older man who intends to marry a younger, poorer woman may want to assure her (or she may want to be assured) of adequate support if they split up.

- Most commonly, couples who marry when either or both already have children may want to keep their property separate to ensure the support and inheritance rights of their children.

B. What goes into a premarital contract?

Many couples want to document all aspects of their relationship in their premarital agreement. We applaud their zeal, but warn that certain provisions are unenforceable and should be kept out.

1. Enforceable provisions

An individualized marriage contract can, in theory, cover any aspect of the marriage relationship, including the division of housework, child care, finances, sexual rights, birth control, children and who feeds the canary. California law allows marital partners to contract regarding any matter, including personal rights and obligations, that does not violate "public policy."[3] For example, parents may not contract away a child's right to support.

Because clauses that deal with most "lifestyle" subjects (like feeding the canary, washing the dishes or taking care of the kids) are not enforced by courts, we do not cover them here.[4] If you want an agreement to cover those issues, we suggest that you write two contracts. In one, you can outline your "lifestyle" arrangements, and use the contract as a guide. The other agreement can settle your property ownership concerns, including income sharing (or not), payment of debts and division of property if you should divorce.

Below is a list of some topics to consider when drawing up a premarital agreement. All of these provisions can be enforced in a court of law. Remember that each couple's situation is unique; provisions relevant to

---

[3]Family Code §1612
[4]*Marriage of Garrity & Bishton* (1986) 181 CA3d 675

your life may have no place in another couple's contract. To illustrate some ways contracts can be used, we include several examples throughout this chapter.

a. Property. You can include provisions that address ownership of property acquired by either spouse before or during marriage, or even for just a portion of the marriage, for example, after the date of the contract. The easiest way to deal with your property is to make three lists and designate property as community, husband's separate or wife's separate. If it's relevant to your marriage, you can also designate who will manage and control certain items of property, such as a family business.

b. Income. One item of property couples often make agreements about is income— wages, capital gains, interest, retirement benefits and similar assets. If both spouses earn income, they might agree to keep their incomes separate.[5]

c. Retirement benefits. Retirement benefits are another item of property many couples make specific provisions for, primarily because court cases declaring retirement benefits (except Social Security) to be community property have made many divorces far more complicated and expensive. The complication and expense arise because retirement plans are difficult to value. In a premarital agreement, spouses can keep their retirement plans separate from the onset of the marriage.

d. Debts. A provision defining and allocating separate and community debts can be included in a marriage contract. Keep in mind, however, that such an agreement would have no effect on creditors if the debt was originally incurred by both spouses. (See Chapter 4.)

e. Estate planning—wills and inheritances. When drafting a marriage contract, you can include provisions specifying what each spouse's will, trust or other document disposing of property at death (called estate planning) will say. In our view, however, this is not wise. Estate planning documents should be flexible and changed as conditions require. A binding contract does away with flexibility. If you do want to include estate planning provisions in a marriage contract, consult a lawyer.

f. Support and living expenses. If either spouse has children from a former marriage, you may want to include a provision specifying from what funds child support is to be paid. Even if you have no children, if you intend to share some expenses and pay others separately, you should specify your intentions. Like the property lists, lists of community expenses, husband's separate expenses and wife's separate expenses can be made to include rent or mortgage, utilities, food, automobile, medical costs, recreation and the like.

Another option—apart from listing who pays for what—is to specify which expenses are to be shared and at what percentages. If both spouses work outside the house, you can pool your incomes and pay proportionately to your incomes. Another possibility is to split the expenses 50-50 and declare whatever is left over to be each spouse's separate property.

However you allocate expenses, you cannot contract away the basic duty to support your spouse for necessaries of life, which include

---

[5] *Marriage of Dawley* (1976) 17 CA3d 342

clothing, food, shelter and medical expenses.[6]

g. Increased earning capacity from education. If one spouse goes to school and increases her ability to earn, the other spouse has no community property interest in this increased earning capacity, although, at divorce, the community (the couple) is entitled to reimbursement for any contribution of community property funds toward the spouse's education.[7] Many couples decide to have more specificity on this subject in their agreement.

2. What you can't agree to— unenforceable provisions

Courts will not enforce marital (pre- or post-marriage) contracts that alter the "essential elements" of the marital relationship or which promote divorce, such as an agreement which gives a spouse a definite financial reward upon divorce.[8] California law also prohibits prenuptial agreement provisions that are unconscionable (grossly unfair)— this essentially means that one spouse did not disclose the extent and nature of her property holdings to the other spouse.[9]

Altering the "essential elements" of marriage. "Violation of public policy" is the reason courts give when refusing to enforce contracts that alter the basic obligations and responsibilities of marriage. As one judge said:

If [married persons could] . . . contract as to the allowance the husband or wife may receive, the number of dresses she may have, the places where they will spend their evenings and *vacations, and innumerable other aspects of their personal relationship . . . [it] would open endless field for controversy and bickering and would destroy the element of flexibility needed in making adjustments to new conditions arising in marital life. There is no reason, of course, why the wife cannot voluntarily pay her husband a monthly sum or the husband, by mutual understanding, quit his job and travel with his wife. The objection is to putting such conduct into a binding contract, tying the parties' hands in the future and inviting controversy and litigation between them.*[10]

The essential obligations of marriage that can't be changed by contract include:

Sexual relations. Courts refuse to enforce contracts in which spouses agree to refrain from sexual intercourse or agree not to have any children.

Spousal support: The spouses' duty to support each other during marriage cannot be contracted away.[11] Thus, if no community property is available to pay for one spouse's necessaries of life—food, shelter, clothing and medical costs—the other spouse's separate property is fair game.

The duty to pay spousal support after marriage is not so clear. The California legislature specifically rejected a bill that would allow couples to waive spousal support, in a premarital or marital contract, in the event they divorced. So while courts will not enforce such provisions, they often enforce reasonable provisions that do provide for spousal support.[12] See *How to Do Your Own Divorce*, Chapter 5, for more information on spousal support.

---

[6]Family Code §4301, 914; *See vs. See* (1966) 64 C2d 778
[7]Family Code §2641
[8]Family Code §1620
[9]Family Code §1615

[10]*Graham vs. Graham* (1940) 33 F.Supp 936,939
[11]Family Code §§720, 914 & 4301
[12]*Marriage of Dawley* (1976) 17 CA3d 342

Child support: Courts reserve all rights to set child support.

Personal services: Contract provisions to reimburse a spouse for personal services (such as housework and domestic services) have been voided by courts on the theory that an implied term of the marriage contract is that these duties are performed by a spouse without compensation. This is an area where ideas are changing, so at some point in the near future we expect such contracts to be honored.

Promoting divorce: It used to be that contracts made with terms for what happens in case of divorce were void as a violation of public policy. The state has been discouraging divorces for so long that courts have taken years to accept the fact that divorces and short-term marriages are best for many people. Thus, courts now enforce contracts made in contemplation of divorce, as long as they do not *promote* divorce. A realistic plan—fairly and freely entered into—preparing for the future, in the event a marriage should end, does not violate public policy and will be enforced. An agreement that gives one spouse a powerful incentive to end the marriage, such as a huge amount of property, probably won't be enforced.[13]

C. Marital property agreements

Like its cousin, the prenuptial agreement, the marital property agreement alters the property rights prescribed by California community property laws. It is, as the name implies, drafted *during* marriage. The same rules which apply to prenuptial agreements, as set out above, apply to marital property agreements.

D. Marital settlement agreements

A marital settlement agreement is used at the end of a marriage or at the onset of a legal separation. It allows the partners to decide issues concerning property, children and support by agreement, rather than by having a judge make decisions based upon state guidelines. We discuss marital settlement agreements further in Chapter 10.

E. How to draft an agreement

Before you draw up any agreement, we strongly recommend that you read this entire book. Until you understand your rights and responsibilities under California's marriage laws, you can't make intelligent decisions about what elements you want to change. You should also:

- Make sure both parties have disclosed all assets, debts, income and expenses and anything else at all that affects the value of the estate, now or in the future. If you aren't completely honest and open with each other, a court could reexamine your agreement far in the future and refuse to enforce its terms.[14]

- Draw up and sign the agreement together, under normal circumstances. Any contract can be challenged if it appears that one party didn't really understand or have any choice about its terms. An agreement handed to a prospective spouse minutes before the wedding, or given with a take-it-or-leave-it ultimatum, is not likely to be enforced.

- Get the advice of a tax specialist on the tax consequences of changing the status of valuable property.

---

[13]*Marriage of Noghrey* (1985) 169 CA3d 326

[14]Family Code §1615

- See separate lawyers if one party is experienced in business affairs and the other is not. Contracts have been set aside if a court decides someone with business sophistication seems to have put something over on someone who was less experienced in business matters.

- Have a lawyer check the contract if it is complex or if a lot of property (now or potentially) is involved.

Premarital and marital agreements must be put in writing and signed by both spouses to be enforceable. In addition, if the agreement (premarital or marital) concerns real estate, your signatures should be notarized and the agreement recorded at the county recorder's office.[15] If you don't record it, the change in property ownership will not be valid as to third parties (creditors, for example) who had no way of knowing that ownership changed.

If you want to make any changes in the agreement after it's signed, you must follow the same formalities required of the original contract—that is, the change or revocation must be in writing and, if the contract con-

[15]Family Code §1502

cerns real estate, it must be notarized and recorded.

F. Sample marriage contracts

We have included sample premarital and marital property agreements here. A sample marital settlement agreement can be found in Nolo's *How to Do Your Own Divorce*, by Ed Sherman.

1. Prenuptial agreements: Agreements made before marriage

Below are two examples of prenuptial contracts that contain clauses addressing several common concerns of couples who plan to marry.

Elvira and John

Elvira is a widow of 67 and John a widower of 70. They both have grown children from first marriages, comfortable nest eggs and fair monthly incomes from freelance activities (Elvira is a paste-up artist and John contributes regularly to a library journal). They want to share the rest of their lives together but feel it unnecessary to embrace California's community property system.

Sample prenuptial contract—Older couple keeping property separate

ELVIRA REDWING and JOHN FLEETFOOT agree as follows:

1. That they will get married on or before _____, 19__.

2. That during their marriage, their finances will be governed by the terms of this agreement.

3. That each clause and sub-clause of this agreement is separate and divisible from the others, and that should a court refuse to enforce one or more clause or sub-clause, the others are still valid and in full force.

4. That the promises of each party are consideration for the promises of the other.

5. That each has fully disclosed his assets and liabilities to the other and each waives any right to further disclosure.

6. That as of the date of this contract, John and Elvira each own various property, and that this property, and all earnings and accumulations which accrue to this property, shall remain separate property. Elvira's separate property is listed in Schedule A of this contract, which is incorporated in and made a part of this agreement; John's separate property is listed in Schedule B of this contract, which is incorporated in and made a part of this agreement. These lists will be kept up to date as property is sold, transferred and accumulated.

7. That all property (real or personal) acquired during marriage by Elvira and John, including but not limited to income from personal services, pensions and retirement plans, shall remain separate property except as provided in clause 9 and that John and Elvira will maintain separate bank and credit accounts.

8. That the monthly living expenses of Elvira and John while they are living together, including food, utilities, housekeeping and gardening expenses, shall be shared equally.

9. That if in the future John and Elvira desire to jointly purchase any real or personal property of a value of $1,000 or more, they shall write a separate agreement to cover that property.

10. a. That John is aware that the bulk of Elvira's separate property stems from the estate of her deceased husband and that Elvira wants this property to descend to her children by her former husband at her death. John respects Elvira's viewpoint and will not assert any rights as husband he might acquire in such separate property.

b. Elvira likewise understands that should John predecease her, he plans to leave his separate property to his children by the use of will, trust and joint ownership investments. Elvira agrees to respect his plan and will likewise not assert whatever rights as wife that she might have in the estate of John after his death.

_____   _____
Date   John Fleetfoot

_____   _____
Date   Elvira Redwing

Ronaldo and Betty

Ronaldo is a 35-year-old salesman who was married and divorced in his twenties. The divorce was drawn-out, nasty and expensive. When it was finally over, he swore he would never go through that again, even if it meant not remarrying. He has a child from his first marriage who lives with his former wife.

Betty and a business partner run a small restaurant. After several years of barely scraping by, they have started making good profits as the restaurant has become popular.

Because Ronaldo and Betty can support themselves and don't plan to have children, they want to keep all their property separate. This also eliminates the potential problems of using Betty's money to pay Ronaldo's child support, or having Ronaldo obtain a community property interest in Betty's business.

Sample prenuptial contract — Younger couple keeping property separate

Ronaldo Meza and Betty Chen agree that:

1. They will get married on or before _____, 19____.

2. During their marriage, their finances will be governed by the terms of this agreement.

3. Each clause of this agreement is separate and divisible from the others; should a court refuse to enforce one or more clause, the others are still valid and in full force.

4. The promises of each are made in consideration of the promises of the other.

5. Each has fully disclosed his assets and liabilities to the other and each waives any right to further disclosure.

6. Ronaldo agrees that all real or personal property acquired by Betty during their marriage will be her separate property. All property means just that, and includes (but is not limited to) profits from her business, any increase in her ability to earn as a result of future education or increase in value of her business interests.

7. Betty agrees that all real or personal property acquired by Ronaldo during their marriage will be his separate property. All property means just that, and includes (but is not limited to) his pension plan, any increase in his ability to earn as a result of future education, and earnings.

8. Betty will not have any responsibility for child support payments to Ronaldo's daughter, Theresa.

9. Betty and Ronaldo will maintain separate checking accounts, own and pay for their own motor vehicles, and will not commingle their separate property in any way.

10. Betty and Ronaldo will each pay one-half of all household expenses, including rent.

11. Should Betty and Ronaldo ever decide to buy a house or other real property together, each will contribute one-half the purchase price and title will be taken in joint tenancy. Each agrees to sign an agreement at that time that the joint tenancy property shall be separate, not community, property.

12. Should Betty and Ronaldo ever divorce, neither will have any obligation to pay the other spousal support. *[This provision is not enforceable; however, it shows intent.]*

_____   _____

Date   Ronaldo Meza

_____   _____

Date   Betty Chen

2. Marital agreements:
Agreements made during marriage

Any issues contained in a prenuptial agreement can be included in a contract entered into during the marriage. Again, the most common area of concern is property ownership. Below are some short sample agreements that illustrate how to clarify or change the status of property.

Sample marital agreement defining separate and community property

1. We, Michael Angelo and Donna Tello, husband and wife, make this agreement on _____, 19___.

2. We have been married since _____, 19___.

3. Each of us makes the promises in this agreement in consideration for the promises of the other.

4. Should a court refuse to enforce any clause of this agreement, the others remain in full force and effect.

5. We both have certain separate property and our interest in community property. We intend to define such property by this agreement.

6. I, Michael Angelo, hereby acknowledge that the following described property is the sole and separate property of my wife and that I have no right, title or interest whatsoever in the property:
[Itemize and describe property]

7. I, Donna Tello, hereby acknowledge that the following described property is the sole and separate property of my husband and that I have no right, title or interest whatsoever in the property:
[Itemize and describe property]

8. We declare that except for the property described in clauses 6 and 7 above, all property of whatever kind now owned by us or standing in the names of either of us is and shall remain our community property. *[Itemize and describe property, if necessary]*

_____
Date

_____
Date

_____
Michael Angelo

_____
Donna Tello

[Notarize and record this contract if any property listed is real estate.]

Sample marital agreement making existing property community property

1. We, Michael Angelo and Donna Tello, husband and wife, make this agreement on _____, 19____.

2. We have been married since _____, 19____.

3. We hereby declare that all the property of whatever kind now owned by us and standing in the record name of either of us on this date is our community property.

4. This agreement is not intended to affect the ownership of property acquired by either of us after the date of this agreement.

_____
Date

_____
Date

_____
Michael Angelo

_____
Donna Tello

[Notarize and record this contract if
any property affected is real estate.]

Sample marital agreement making all property community property

1. We, Michael Angelo and Donna Tello, husband and wife, make this agreement on _____, 19____.   .

2. We have been married since _____, 19____.

3. We hereby declare that all property of whatever kind now held by us and all property that shall hereafter be acquired by either of us from whatever source shall be our community property.

_____
Date

_____
Date

_____
Michael Angelo

_____
Donna Tello

[Notarize and record this contract if
any property affected is real estate.]

Sample marital agreement changing certain community property to separate property

1. We, Michael Angelo and Donna Tello, husband and wife, make this agreement on _____, 19____.

2. We have been married since _____, 19____.

3. We own the following described community property. It is our desire to divide such property equally between us:

[Itemize and describe property]

4. We agree that from this date on, half of the property *[Itemize and describe property]* shall be the separate property of Michael Angelo and one-half of the property *[Itemize and describe property]* shall be the separate property of Donna Tello.

_____   _____

Date   Michael Angelo

_____   _____

Date   Donna Tello

[Notarize and record this contract if
any property affected is real estate.]

Sample marital agreement changing all community property to separate property

---

1. We, Michael Angelo and Donna Tello, husband and wife, make this agreement on _____, 19___.

2. We have been married since _____, 19___.

3. We have the following community property:

[Itemize and describe property]

4. We desire to make a settlement of all of our property rights so that each of us will own approximately one-half of the property as his or her separate property. We agree that from this date the following property will be the separate property of Michael Angelo:

[Itemize and describe property]

We also agree that the following property will be the separate property of Donna Tello:

[Itemize and describe property]

5. We agree that all property hereafter acquired by either of us including earnings shall be the separate property of the one so acquiring it.

6. We understand that but for this agreement the earnings and income from the personal services of the other spouse would be community property, but that by this agreement such earnings are made separate.

_____
Date

_____
Michael Angelo

_____
Date

_____
Donna Tello

[Notarize and record this contract if
any property listed is real estate.]

As discussed in Chapter 3, determining how title to property is held is a beginning step in determining the ownership and status of property. The following are two sample agreements to be used when changing the title of property.

Sample marital agreement changing title to personal property

Pauline and Don Chin agree as follows:

1. Since 1970, Don has owned a 1955 vintage Ford Fairlane.

2. As of the date of this agreement, Don intends to make a gift of one-half of the car to Pauline, and Don waives his right to be reimbursed for his separate property contribution should Don and Pauline later divorce.

3. Don has written to the Department of Motor Vehicles to request that the car registration be changed from "Don Chin" to "Don and Pauline Chin" as joint tenants, and it is Don's intention that from the date of this agreement forward that Don and Pauline own the Ford Fairlane in joint tenancy.

_____   _____
Date   Don Chin

_____   _____
Date   Pauline Chin

[It is not imperative that Pauline sign this agreement,
but it can't hurt.]

Sample marital agreement changing title to real property

I, Frances Miller, hereby give my joint tenancy interest in our family cabin located near Big Bear Lake, in California, to my husband, Thomas Miller, as his separate property.

_____   _____
Date   Frances Miller

[Because this statement concerns real property, notarize and record
it at the county recorder's office where the property is located,
along with a new deed reflecting the ownership change.]

Because very few items of property carry a deed, registration or title certificate, you may need to draft agreements to change the status of property not having a title document. The following are two sample agreements setting forth ownership transfers for property having no title.

Sample marital agreement transferring ownership of earnings

```
    We, Judy and Leroy Dubois, hereby agree that from this date for-
ward our earnings and other employment benefits will be the separate
property of the spouse who earned them.




_____                    _____
Date                                   Judy Dubois

_____                    _____
Date                                   Leroy Dubois
```

Sample marital agreement transferring ownership of inheritance

```
    I, Frances Miller, hereby deposit the $5,000 I inherited as sepa-
rate property from my Uncle Mickey into the community property bank
account number 555-123456, located at the First Bank of St. Thomas,
which I own jointly with my husband, Thomas Miller. I intend that
this inheritance now be owned by Thomas and me as community property.



_____                    _____
Date                                   Frances Miller
```

Caution—agreements may be challenged. Agreements to change title to or ownership of property may later be challenged at divorce on the ground that one party didn't adequately understand what was happening and was unfairly influenced to surrender valuable rights to the other. Especially if the property involved in the ownership or title change is extremely valuable and if one spouse has more business sophistication than the other, the spouse who is giving up valuable property should consult briefly with an attorney, and note the consultation in the agreement, just so the agreement will not be vulnerable to this kind of attack.

Spouses often combine separate and community property, and may want an agreement showing their intent. Here are some sample agreements on combining property which will help you get your understandings down on paper.

Sample marital agreement combining real property

Diane and Danny Huntcol agree as follows:

1. Diane owns a piece of land at 2300 E. 12th St., Oakland, California.

2. Danny and Diane plan to contribute community property funds and a lot of their own labor to build a house on Diane's land.

3. Danny and Diane will both own the house even though it is situated on Diane's land. If the house is sold, one spouse dies or the couple divorces, Diane is entitled to the value of the land plus the value of one-half of all improvements, and Danny is entitled to one-half the value of all improvements.

4. Title to the property will be transferred from Diane to Danny and Diane as tenants in common and a new deed will be recorded.

_____
Date

_____
Date

_____
Danny Huntcol

_____
Diane Huntcol

[This agreement and a new deed should be notarized and recorded at the county recorder's office where the property is located.]

Sample marital agreement combining real property

John and Sandy Kerensky agree as follows:

1. That they're joint owners of a duplex apartment building which they hold as tenants in common.

2. That John contributed 80 percent of the money to purchase the building from his separate property and that Sandy contributed the remaining 20 percent from their community property.

3. That upon sale of the building, John will be entitled to 90 percent of the money received, and that Sandy will receive 10 percent.

_____   _____
Date   Sandy Kerensky

_____   _____
Date   John Kerensky

*[This agreement and a new deed should be notarized and recorded
at the county recorder's office where the property is located.]*

Sample marital agreement combining personal property with title document

Patricia and Zeke Poulos agree as follows:

1. That Patricia owns a 1967 model Chris-Craft cruiser valued at $40,000.

2. That the engine in the boat is shot and that Zeke is willing to put $10,000 of his money into the boat to make it seaworthy for a trip.

3. That in exchange for his $10,000 investment, Patricia hereby transfers to Zeke a 1/5 (20%) interest in the boat.

4. Should Zeke or Patricia wish to sell their share at any time, they must give the other 90 days' notice. During this time, the non-selling spouse may buy the interest of the other for its fair market value, which will be determined by appraisal if the couple can't agree. If, after ninety days, one spouse hasn't bought the other out, the boat will be placed for sale on the open market and the proceeds divided 80% to Patricia and 20% to Zeke.

5. The title slip to the boat will be changed from Patricia to Patricia and Zeke as tenants in common and the Department of Motor Vehicles will be notified.

_____   _____
Date   Patricia Poulos

_____   _____
Date   Zeke Poulos

Sample marital agreement combining personal property with title document

Jeanne and Wilfred Park agree as follows:

1. That they are buying a 1990 Mercedes-Benz automobile using 50 percent community property and 50 percent Jeanne's separate property, which she received from her Aunt Lucy as a gift.

2. That the Mercedes-Benz belongs one-fourth to Wilfred and three-fourths to Jeanne, and that, if the car is ever sold, the money received for the sale will be divided following these percentages.

3. That the title slip to the car will indicate that Wilfred and Jeanne own the car as tenants in common.

_____   _____
Date   Jeanne Park

_____   _____
Date   Wilfred Park

Sample marital agreement combining personal property without title document

Shyam and Nata Divan agree as follows:

1. That Shyam owns a collection of four (4) antique record player cabinets valued at $6,000.

2. That Nata is willing to put in time and approximately $650 worth of materials to repair and refinish these cabinets to make them ready for sale.

3. That Nata will be responsible for the advertising and sale of these cabinets.

4. That upon sale of the cabinets, Shyam will be entitled to 75% of the money received, and that Nata will receive 25%.

_____   _____
Date   Shyam Divan

_____   _____
Date   Nata Divan

6
Children

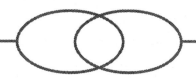

"Love and marriage go together like a horse and carriage." So goes the song which seemed to be written indelibly across the psyche of the nation a generation or two ago. Looking back on those years, the only change we might suggest is to add the word "baby" before "carriage." Certainly, marriage and babies seemed to be inseparable as the population of the United States jumped from 122 million in 1930 to over twice that today.

Issues covered in other chapters:

Child custody, visitation and child support during and after divorce is discussed in Chapter 7.

A. Who are the child's biological parents?—Paternity

Hallelujah! California no longer uses the words "legitimate" and "illegitimate" to describe children. The law now says "the parent and child relationship extends equally to every child and to every parent, regardless of the marital status of the parents."[1] It's about time, too.

Even though "legitimate" and "illegitimate" are no longer used to describe the marital status of a child's parents, it is still important legally to know who a child's biological parents are. Inheritance, child custody, support, visitation, adoption and many other laws specify the rights and duties of parents. Then there's the importance of having a coherent medical history.

1. Paternity

While it's normally not difficult to figure out who a child's biological mother is, identify-ing fathers isn't always so easy. California law gives rules to establish whether a parent-child relationship exists.[2] These rules are somewhat complicated, but in a broad sense they provide that a man is *presumed* to be the father of a child in any of the following circumstances:

Circumstance 1. The man is married to the mother when the child is born, or was married to her within 300 days of the child's birth. Even if the man dies, or he and the mother divorce while she is pregnant, he is still presumed to be the father.

Circumstance 2. The man and the mother, before the child's birth, attempted to get married—got a license and had a ceremony—but the marriage wasn't valid for some reason, such as one partner was still married to someone else, *and* the child was born during the attempted marriage period or within 300 days after its termination.

Circumstance 3. After the child's birth, the man and the mother marry (or attempt to marry), even if the marriage is later annulled, *and*

- The man consents to being named father on the birth certificate; *or*

- The man signs a written agreement to support the child or is ordered by a court to do so.

Circumstance 4. The man receives the child into his home and openly holds out the child as his natural child. The man cannot be denied the right to become a presumed father by the mother's keeping the child from him.[3]

---

[1] Family Code §7602

[2] Family Code §§7600–7730 (The Uniform Parentage Act)
[3] *In Re Adoption of Kelsey S.* (1992) 1 C4th 816

Circumstance 5. The child is born outside the United States and the man signs a declaration under penalty of perjury acknowledging that he is the father.[4]

You will note that these rules deal with presumptions. This means that a certain fact situation is presumed to produce a certain legal conclusion, unless rebutted by stronger evidence.[5] For example, in Circumstance 4, if a man takes a child into his home and says that he is the father, even though he never married the child's mother, he is legally presumed to be the father. This doesn't mean that he *is* the father—he might still be able to rebut the presumption; that is, prove with clear and convincing evidence that even though he received a child into his home and told his friends and family that he was the father, in fact, he was not.

In addition, a man will not be permitted to assert his status as a presumed father in Circumstance 2, 3, 4 or 5 if:

- The child was conceived as a result of rape and the man was convicted of that crime; or

- The child was conceived as a result of "unlawful sexual intercourse," the man was convicted of that crime, and the mother was under age 15 and the man was over 21.

One law, however, creates an exception to the rule allowing paternity presumptions to be rebutted. It says:

The child of a wife cohabiting with her husband, who is not impotent or sterile, is conclusively presumed to be a child of the marriage.[6]

This nonrebuttable presumption has produced some bizarre cases, including some where the racial characteristics of the child were obviously different from those of the mother's husband. For this and other reasons, the legislature modified the presumption to allow a husband, a man claiming to be the father or the child through a guardian, to challenge the husband's status as father within two years of the child's birth if blood tests indicate that the husband is not the father.[7] Recent advances in blood testing make it easy to disprove paternity, and possible to prove paternity with 98% certainty (or more).

If the issue is not raised within the two-year period, the presumption can no longer be rebutted.[8] The time period is short because courts are very concerned with preserving the matrimonial family. In one case, for example, the lover of the child's mother proved with 98% accuracy that he was the father of the child. The California court rejected his claim because the mother was married to another man at the time and the court felt the "integrity of the matrimonial family" outweighed any claim to fatherhood by the lover. A very divided United States Supreme Court upheld the decision.[9] More recently, a California court has found that the conclusive presumption is unconstitutional when applied to a marital relationship which ended eight days after the child's birth.[10] This is an area of law still changing, and will likely continue to change as the definition and structure of families evolve.

---

[4]Family Code §7611(e)—This provision will become ineffective January 1, 1997
[5]*In Re Olivia H.* (1987) 196 CA3d 325
[6]Family Code §7540

[7]Family Code §§7550–7557
[8]*Michelle Marie W. vs. Ronald W.* (1985) 39 CA3d 354
[9]*Michael H. vs. Gerald D.* (1989) 491 US 110—The Court left open the possibility that the presumption might still be unconstitutional as applied to substantially different facts.
[10]*In Re Melissa G.* (1989) 213 CA3d 1082

2. What if the father will not acknowledge paternity?

Whenever there is a paternity issue, the court may on its own motion or at the request of any person whose blood is involved (mother, child, father) order any or all of the parties to submit to blood tests in order to establish paternity. If a party refuses to submit to the blood tests the court has ordered, that refusal is admissible in evidence on the paternity issue and the court may resolve the issue against the party who has refused to comply, or enforce the original order for blood tests if the interests of justice require.[11] Paternity disputes can be costly and humiliating. See a specialist attorney or call your local district attorney's office for help.

3. Alternative insemination

When a married woman has a child by alternative (sometimes called "artificial") insemination, and becomes impregnated with semen from someone other than her husband, her husband is nevertheless irrebuttably presumed to be the father and the sperm donor has no rights. (The husband's consent must be in writing signed by him and his wife.)[12] The law prefers "intact" families and does not want the donor to come along and disrupt things, nor does it want the husband to fail to support the children. In California, if the insemination procedure for an unmarried woman is performed by a licensed physician, the donor is not considered the father.[13] If a licensed physician is not used, the donor may be considered the father.

4. Surrogacy and in vitro fertilization

In vitro fertilization is the fertilization of a human egg outside the human body. Through this process an egg can be removed from one woman, fertilized in the laboratory with the intended father's sperm, and then implanted in the uterus of a *different* woman, who gives birth to the child. This process allows a woman who is unable to carry a fetus the opportunity to have a child of her own egg.

The legal question for in vitro fertilization is whether the egg donor or the child bearer is the biological mother of the child. The California Supreme Court reasoned[14] that maternity can be established by the act of giving birth *or* by blood tests.[15] Two biological mothers can be established by such tests, but the court rejected the suggestion that a child may have two natural mothers, so it resolved the conflict by looking to the intent of the surrogacy contract. The court concluded that if the egg donor and the child bearer do not coincide in one woman, the parties' intention, as expressed in the surrogacy contract, will be determinative. This means that the woman

---

[11]Family Code §7551
[12]Family Code §7613(a)
[13]Family Code §7613

[14]*Johnson vs. Calvert* (1993) 5 C4th 84
[15]Family Code §7650

who was intended to raise the child as her own, under the terms of the contract, will be considered the child's biological mother under California law.

Surrogacy. The situation above is to be distinguished from a surrogacy arrangement, where the surrogate provides both the egg and womb. Upon birth of the child, the surrogate mother relinquishes all rights in and responsibilities for the child and turns the child over to the man, whose wife formally adopts the child.

In surrogacy, the surrogate is undeniably the biological mother of the child, but the legal question is whether she can be compelled to perform her contractual promise to consent to the adoption of the child by the intended mother after birth.

You are undoubtedly aware of the *Case of Baby M* that was much in the news. In that case, the surrogate mother refused to give up custody of the child after she was born. The New Jersey Supreme Court ruled that the surrogate contract was unenforceable, declared the surrogate mother the natural mother, and then decided the case as it would any other disputed custody case. Although *Baby M* is not controlling in California, California courts may look to it for guidance.

If you're planning to have a child by any type of surrogate method, you should definitely see a lawyer who is a specialist in that field.

B. The duty to support children

Parents have a civil duty to support their children.[16] The primary method of enforcing child support obligations is through a lawsuit brought by the custodial parent or by the district attorney on behalf of the Department of Social Services, if the child receives AFDC benefits. Nonsupport is also a crime, punishable by a jail sentence and a fine.[17]

While the duty to support historically fell on the father, California obligates both the *father and mother* to support their children. A parent who *willfully* fails to fulfill the obligation may be prosecuted by the district attorney's office. It makes no difference whether or not the child's parents were ever married; however, any court-ordered child support arising from a divorce or paternity action takes precedence over the general legal duty to support.

Example

Grady and Karen married and had three children. They separate for a year and share custody of the children. Both have a legal duty to support the children. Eventually, they divorce and agree on joint custody, the details of which are to be worked out. Karen makes three times as much money as Grady does; the court orders her to support the children during the months that she has custody and to pay Grady $100 per month per child for the months that he has them. This court order takes precedence over their general duty to support their children.

Parents who have no income or savings or can't find work are not guilty of failing to support. It is a crime only to *willfully* fail to support your children. A court, however, in determining the ability to support, will consider all income—including Social Security, unemployment, pension payments, welfare and other benefits—in deciding if there is enough money to take care of the kids. In addition, a nonsupporting parent may be ordered at the request of the custodial parent to submit to a vocational exami-

---

[16]Family Code §3900

[17]Penal Code §§270, 271(a)

nation to determine his or her ability to work, or be required to submit a list of places he or she has applied for work.[18]

Example

John is the sole support of his wife and children. After his marriage failed, he quit his job as a police officer and went back to school to become a social worker. John could no longer support his ex-wife and children, who now applied for welfare. A judge might be sympathetic to his desire to change careers, but not to his failure to support. The judge would surely require John to support the family, perhaps even based on his level of earnings when he worked as a police officer.

Parents are also obligated to accept their child into their home, or to provide alternative shelter when required to do so by a child protective agency. This law makes it is illegal to abandon or desert your child.[19]

C. Neglect, abuse and losing children to foster care

Supporting a child is not enough. Parents must also refrain from abusing or neglecting their children. Generally, child abuse is broadly defined by statute to include a parent's failure to provide adequate shelter, food, clothing, medical treatment, etc. The government has a significant interest in protecting children, and so the legislature has enacted severe criminal penalties for child abuse. Practically speaking, child protective workers give broad latitude to how parents raise their children and won't interfere unless they receive a report indicating abuse, neglect or lack of parental control (see Section D below.)

If a child is abused or neglected, the Child Protective Services (CPS) of the California

Department of Social Services (DSS) may try to have the kids removed from the home through a dependency hearing; parents are entitled to have an attorney appointed to represent them. The CPS worker will try to work out an arrangement for reunification at a prehearing conference. A reunification arrangement usually requires the parents to attend parenting classes and some kind of therapy sessions. If the parent agrees to the arrangement, he, she or they must sign a reunification plan. If the parents and CPS can't negotiate an agreement, or the parents want to dispute charges, the parents can request a formal hearing before a Juvenile Court judge.

If the children are taken away, they are put into foster homes.[20] During this period, the parents will want to act quickly to get their children back and do whatever the court has ordered as condition for reunification. For the first 12 months of separation, the court presumes it is in the children's best interest to be reunited with their parents. Between 12 and 18 months, the presumption decreases. At 18 months, the court presumes that "stability" is in the children's best interest—stability is defined as staying in the foster placement. If reunification is not progressing at the end of the 12- or 18-month period, the judge will make an order of permanent foster care or guardianship (in which case the parents will have the right to stay in touch with the children), or adoption (in which case parental rights are terminated; see Section E below).

---

[18]Family Code §4505
[19]Penal Code §270.5

[20]Welfare and Institutions Code §202 states that when a child is removed from his or her home, the state must give the child a home as good as the one the natural parents should provide. Sad to say, however, standards of care in some foster homes and juvenile centers in California are miserable. We have seen situations where a child is taken out of an admittedly bad home and then placed in a worse one.

When children are in foster care, DSS often seeks reimbursement of the foster care costs and legal fees from parents. Usually, DSS won't pursue parents on welfare, but will try for some reimbursement if the parents have any non-welfare income.

The incidence of child abuse in this country is horrifying. Abused children are often the voices never heard. As a parent you are entrusted with the care and welfare of your child. If you unable to deal with the stresses and difficulties of parenthood and find yourself treating your children badly, please realize that there are many good programs available which can help you and perhaps save your children.

For more information or help contact:

Child Crisis Service
(415) 558-8484

or

The TALK Line
(415) 441-KIDS

Additional organizations that can help are listed in Chapter 9.

D. "I can't control my kids!" Delinquents

Parents are also required to keep their children within their control. This doesn't mean you must know where your kids are at all times and account for their every action, but it does mean that if your daughter is picked up by the police for tossing a brick into a bicycle shop window, she may be declared "beyond parental control." As we said above if a child is "beyond parental control" CPS may try to have the kids removed from the home. If your child is taken away, he or she will be placed in a juvenile detention center.

The Juvenile Court also has the authority to exercise informal probation when it appears that a child is headed for trouble. This will only be done with the cooperation of the parent and child. The CPS worker will attempt to help the parent and the child work through their problems in a positive way, perhaps by getting them involved in community programs. The time to use this program, which bypasses all the court hearings, lawyers, formal reports and reunification plans is before, not after, real trouble develops.

We don't have the space here to explain all the laws relating to juveniles. Go to your county law libraries or to the main (or a large) branch of your public library. Ask a librarian to help you find the Welfare and Institutions Code, which contains most laws pertaining to minors and their welfare.

E. Adoptions

This is a court procedure whereby an adult or adults assume(s) a parent-child relationship with the natural child[21] of another. The adopting parent(s) assume(s) full legal responsibility for the child, including the legal duty to support. The natural parent(s), assuming that they are alive, are legally eliminated from any relationship with the child. This means that an adopted child inherits from his or her adoptive parents and their family just as if he or she was a natural child, but would not inherit from his or her natural parents, should they die without a will.

---

[21]Family Code §9300—Adoption of one adult by another is also possible.

If a married person wants to adopt, both the husband and wife must consent; one can't adopt without the other. Single parent adoptions are legally possible and becoming more common. Adoptions by gay couples are rare, although they are happening with more frequency For more information on gay adoptions, see Nolo's *A Legal Guide for Lesbian and Gay Couples.*

Adoption is a weighty step to take. It is a tremendous legal, financial and moral commitment to another human being. Unless you are absolutely sure that you want to raise and support the child, don't adopt. You can divorce a spouse, but you can't divorce a kid. Adoption can be very beneficial for a child because it creates the legal basis for a stable parent-child relationship. If you're an adult taking care of someone else's child and want some legal recognition, however, weigh an adoption against a guardianship. (See Section F below.)

Common questions many people have about adoption include:

- "I will be 45 years old next month; am I too old to adopt?"

- "I have a juvenile arrest; does this mean I can't adopt?"

- "My wife is deaf; will they hold that against us?"

- "Ten years ago I placed my own child up for adoption; does this disqualify me from adopting?"

The answer to all these questions is a qualified "No." We say qualified because this sort of information and a lot more will be considered in deciding whether or not it is in the best interests of the particular child for you to adopt him or her. No one fact (except,

perhaps, a history of child abuse or molestation) will either qualify you or disqualify you.

Adoptions of children fall into four basic categories. We cover each briefly. For more information on adoptions, visit your county law library, and ask the law librarian for assistance.

1. Stepparent adoption

A stepparent adoption occurs when the parent with custody of a child marries a new spouse and the new spouse wants to adopt the child . Without an adoption, the new spouse, called a stepparent, has no legal responsibility for the child, even though he or she may lovingly and competently perform all the parental duties that a natural parent would normally perform. Stepparent adoptions are the most common type of adoption. You can do one yourself with Nolo's *How to Adopt Your Stepchild in California.*

If a stepparent wants to adopt, and the custodial parent and the child (if he or she is old enough to have an opinion) agree, the next thing to do is deal with the noncustodial parent (the other legal parent). If the parent has died, there is obviously no need to be concerned. Any child adopted by a stepparent after the natural parent dies can still keep any Social Security benefits stemming from the account of the deceased parent.

You may be unsure whether or not the child has a legal father. If the parents were never married, don't assume that the child doesn't. Paternity and fatherhood are covered in Section A, above. If the child has a legal father, he must be notified of an adoption and his objections (if any) will be considered by the court.[22]

Assuming the child has a legally recognized noncustodial parent, either of the following must happen before an adoption can take place:

• The noncustodial parent must consent to the adoption and sign a consent form before a County Clerk or a probation worker, if in California, or a notary public, if outside California.

• The noncustodial parent must have abandoned the child. This means that he or she has willfully failed to communicate with the child *and* has failed to pay for the care, support and education of the child in question, when able to do so, for a period of one year or more.

If you file a petition in Superior Court for a stepparent adoption, your case will be referred to a county agency to investigate and write a report for the judge. A social worker will visit your home to talk with the natural parent, prospective adoptive parent and child, if he or she is old enough. Don't worry about the visit. The county isn't looking to dig up dirt; it likes stepparent adoptions. The social worker just wants to make sure there's a stable and loving home. Keep in mind that a

judge won't approve an adoption if the county submits a negative report.

Let us repeat: don't worry about the social worker's visit. Every family has problems. None of us has a perfect family, even though we often waste a lot of energy trying to convince our neighbors that we do. If something in your life might weigh against you in an adoption, such as a bad conduct discharge from the military, a past drinking or a credit problem, it is usually best to be frank with the social worker. She'll probably learn of the skeletons anyway and we have found that old bones don't rattle as much if you bring them out of the closet yourself. After all, in a stepparent adoption, you are already living with the child and probably exercising parental authority, so the department has little motive to reject your petition.

Assuming the county report is favorable, the next step is to go to court and have the judge grant her approval. This is pretty much a formality, with handshakes all around, and the adoptive parent assuring the judge that he will assume full legal responsibility for the child and, as well, provide the love and care so necessary to all children. If the child is over 12 years old, he or she must also consent to the adoption.

As part of an adoption proceeding, the child may be given a new name (often the last name of the adopting father). This is not required, however, and the child can keep his or her original surname. Also, the state will issue a new birth certificate with the new name, if desired. If the child was born outside of California, you can probably get the state of birth to issue a new birth certificate. If the child was born outside the United States, however, it is usually impossible.

---

[22]*Michael U. vs. Jaime B.* (1985) 39 CA3d 787

2. Agency Adoption

An agency adoption occurs when a licensed adoption agency places a child in the home of an adopting parent or parents. The agency gets a full relinquishment of the rights from the natural parents before putting the child up for adoption, so there are normally no worries about a natural parent later surfacing to try and claim "his or her child."

Generally, the adoptive parents must be at least 10 years older than the child. There is no upper age limit or rules concerning physical or mental disabilities for the prospective parents, but adoption agencies usually have their own policies. Indeed, as birth control, family size and changing societal attitudes toward "legitimacy" have reduced the pool of children available for adoption, agencies have become very selective in choosing adoptive parents.

Prospective adoptive parents must file a petition in Superior Court and the adoption must be approved by a judge. If the child is over 12, he or she must consent to the adoption. A county social worker will investigate the family (see Section 1 above) and submit a report to the judge. The standards applied in agency adoptions are stricter than in stepparent adoptions because, unlike stepparent adoptions, the child has had no relationship with the adoptive parents.

Most reputable adoption agencies charge high fees. Part of this money pays for the investigation to determine whether or not the prospective parents are suitable. Adoption agencies prefer that the adoptive parents retain their own lawyer to prepare and present the necessary paperwork to the judge.

3. County Adoption

In a county adoption, children in the care of the county are placed for adoption. In some cases the natural parents consent to the adoption, while in others a judge first terminates parental rights because the parents have abandoned the children or have been found to be unfit parents. Most of these adoptions grow out of foster placements.

Through this program (sometimes called Fost-Adopt), it is now possible for prospective adoptive parents to get on a county list, foster parent and then adopt the child. Keep in mind, however, that the children available through the county program are often not healthy newborns. Many are disabled, abused or emotionally disturbed older children. Many infants coming through the program have been born to drug abusers. They may not be drug-addicted themselves, but the long-term effects of drug addiction at birth are still largely unknown.

In addition, Fost-Adopting leaves the adoptive parents vulnerable to the possibility that a reunification will occur. Reunification with the birth parents is presumed to be in the child's best interest for the first 12–18 months of the placement. Often, the natural parents rehabilitate themselves sufficiently to regain custody of their children.

At the same time, however, if the parents are unable to get their act together, you will be first in line to adopt. The costs are low, and given that you've already been approved as foster parents, your approval to adopt will be easy. Of course, not to be overlooked is the fact that the children in these programs are in desperate need of loving caring parents.

4. Private Adoption

It is possible to adopt a child without going through an adoption agency or the county. These are called "private" or "independent" adoptions. When you read about "baby for sale" scandals, this is the type of adoption involved. Although most private adoptions are carried out honestly and fairly, abuses do crop up now and then. Things have been better in recent years as the state has regulated this area more closely.

When a child is located for private adoption, it is essential that the mother and father sign a consent form. If the identity of the father isn't certain, all possible candidates should sign. Of course, if no one has the foggiest idea who the father is, it is not necessary to get a signature. Even if a parent will not consent to an adoption, the adoption may still be possible if the parent has abandoned the child.[23]

Like other adoptions, private adoptions require that you file a petition with the Superior Court and that a county social worker be appointed to investigate. You will need an attorney's help in preparing the papers, and possibly to advise you on how to deal with the social worker. You can expect a strict investigation. After all, the child is not already in your home, as in the stepparent situation, nor has an agency or the county already investigated you.

You must be 10 years older than the child, but there are no other rules as to mental or physical capability. If you are (or were ever) married, the social worker will want to see your marriage certificate and, if applicable, your final decree of divorce. You also need a certified copy of the child's birth certificate,

the marriage and divorce records of the child's natural parents and whatever else the social worker thinks is relevant. It is very important that the social worker recommend that the adoption take place.

If the county approves the adoption and the court grants it, the child is yours. The child will be given your last name if you desire and you can have the birth certificate reissued. If you are considering a private adoption, make sure you get expert advice to ensure that your rights are protected and that the adoption is handled appropriately.

F. Who will care for our children if something happens to us? Guardianships

For a variety of reasons, minors may live temporarily or even permanently with adults other than their parents. You may take care of someone else's child—maybe a niece, nephew, grandchild or even a friend's child. Or, you may leave your own child with another adult, perhaps while you are away for an extended period of time.

In California, at least one adult must be legally responsible for a minor. You can use a guardianship to fulfill this requirement. A

---

[23]Family Code §7822

guardianship is the legal recognition that an adult other than a legal parent has custody of, and is responsible for, a minor. The guardian takes care of the minor's physical well-being—provides food and shelter, and attends to the minor's education and health-care needs. In some cases, it also means that the guardian manages the minor's assets—money and other property.

Don't confuse guardianship and adoption; they are quite different. When a minor is adopted, the adoptive parent becomes the legal parent of the child. The biological parent loses all parental rights and obligations, including the obligation to support. When a minor has a guardian, the legal relationship between the biological parent and the child remains intact. The biological parent is legally obligated to support the child, and if that parent dies without a will, the child will inherit his or her property.

In California, a *legal* guardianship can be obtained only by:

- Filing legal papers with a court;

- Notifying certain agencies;

- Notifying certain relatives of the minor;

- Appearing before a judge; and

- Being appointed guardian by the court.

In the real world, however, parents make informal arrangements with other adults to care for their children for a specific or even indefinite period of time. Usually these arrangements work just fine, but occasionally situations arise in which the caretaking adult isn't authorized to act—for example, authorizing medical treatment or obtaining benefits for the minor. (See Section G below.)

An adult taking care of a minor who isn't her child will, sooner or later, need to obtain a legal guardianship. *The Guardianship Book*, published by Nolo Press, gives detailed information on how to obtain a legal guardianship.

Note to stepparents: A stepparent who cares for his stepchild may suddenly find himself lacking the legal authority to seek medical care or to enroll his stepchild in school if someone inquires about his legal relationship to the child. If you're a stepparent, it is imperative that you possess an authorization from your spouse like the sample below.

G. Can caretakers give medical consent in an emergency? Parental authorization

What if you're planning a trip for a relatively short period (let's say up to three months), and can't take your child with you? Or what if you're taking care of a friend's child while she is out of the country on business? Or what if you regularly care for a child (such as a stepchild), but are not in a position to become a legal guardian because the legal parent also cares for the child?

In these situations, it isn't possible or practical to go to court and appoint a legal guardian. But if the minor needs medical treatment or wants to attend a school event and the biological parent can't consent, the caretaking adult must. To facilitate this, the parent and other adult need a document spelling out their arrangement. Below we give you a sample document; we suggest you have it notarized. If the caretaking adult and parent anticipate any extraordinary activity for the child (such as taking her out of the country), we suggest that you include specific authorization in the document, or have the parent write a letter to the caretaking adult authorizing the extraordinary activity.

Although the document below uses the word "guardianship," it is not a substitute for a legal guardianship. As stated above, a legal guardianship may be obtained only by going to court.

GUARDIANSHIP AUTHORIZATION

MINOR'S NAME: _____

BIRTHDATE: _____ AGE: _____ YEAR IN SCHOOL: _____

MOTHER'S NAME: _____

ADDRESS: _____

PHONE (HOME): _____ (WORK): _____

FATHER'S NAME: _____

ADDRESS: _____

PHONE (HOME): _____ (WORK): _____

GUARDIAN'S NAME: _____

ADDRESS: _____

PHONE (HOME): _____ (WORK): _____

RELATIONSHIP OF GUARDIAN TO MINOR: _____

IN CASE OF EMERGENCY, IF GUARDIAN CANNOT BE REACHED, CONTACT:

_____

PHONE (HOME): _____ (WORK): _____

Authorization and Consent by Parent(s)

1. I hereby affirm that the minor indicated above is my child and that I have legal custody of her/him. I give my full authorization and consent for my child to live with _____ [name of guardian], or for _____ [name of guardian] to set a place of residence for my child.

2. I give _____ [name of guardian] permission to act in my place and make necessary decisions regarding my child pertaining to any school, educational or religious event including but not limited to enrollment, permission for activities and consent for medical treatment at school.

3. I give _____ [name of guardian] permission to authorize medical and or dental care for my child, including but not limited to medical examinations, X-rays, tests, anesthetic, surgical

operations, hospital care or other treatments that in his/her sole opinion are needed or useful for my child. Such medical treatment shall only be provided upon the advice of and supervision by a physician, surgeon or dentist or other medical practitioner licensed to practice in the United States.

4. This authorization shall cover the following period: from _____, 19__ to _____, 19__.

5. During the period when _____ [name of guardian] cares for my child, the costs of my child's upkeep, living expenses, medical and/or dental expenses shall be paid as follows:

_____

_____

_____

I declare under penalty of perjury under the laws of the State of California that the foregoing is true and correct. Executed this _____ day of _____, 19__ at _____, California.

Mother's Signature: _____

Father's Signature: _____

[NOTARIZATION]

Consent of Guardian

I solemnly affirm that I will assume full responsibility for the minor who will live with me during the period designated above. I agree to make necessary decisions and to provide consent for the minor as set forth in the above Authorization and Consent by Parent(s). I also agree to the terms of the costs of the minor's upkeep, living expenses, medical and/or dental expenses set forth in the above Authorization and Consent by Parent(s).

I declare under penalty of perjury under the laws of the State of California that the foregoing is true and correct. Executed this _____ day of _____, 19__ at _____, California.

Guardian's Signature: _____

[NOTARIZATION]

H. "So my kid broke the window... why should I pay?" Responsibility of parents for the acts of their children

As a general rule, parents are not financially responsible for the acts of their children that cause damage to someone or someone's property. This means that if your child is negligent (for example, trips over her shoe-laces and falls on your neighbor's begonia plant) you are not *legally* required to pay for a new begonia even though it might be polite (and worth thousands in good-neigh-bor relations) to do so.

But (and this is a *big* but) if your child *willfully* damages another's property (little Susie *intentionally* rips up the begonias) you will be responsible for up to $25,000 for each intentional act.[24] And if your child (or a child you are legally responsible for) uses paint or a similar product to deface another's property, you will also be on the hook for court costs and attorney's fees, in addition to the $25,000.[25] If the child causes injury to a person, damages are limited to that person's medical, dental and hospital expenses. Parents! Check your liability insurance!

The parent or guardian having control of the child is liable. If both parents have custody and control, each parent is liable for the full $25,000. A parent without physical custody, who is not exercising actual control over the child when the willful act occurs, cannot be held liable.[26]

What is a "willful" act as opposed to a "neg-ligent" one? "Willful misconduct" is pretty much figured case by case. Most accidental or clumsy acts by children won't constitute willful misconduct, but if the act is semi-delinquent, and especially if the parents knew about the behavior and didn't stop it, liability is likely to be found.[27]

Guns raise the ante of liability and responsi-bility (not just legally). Any injury, caused by a child less than 18 years old, with a gun that a parent let the child have, *or left where she could get it,* can cost the parent up to $30,000 for the death or injury of one person or his property, or $60,000 for the deaths of or injuries to more than one per-son.[28] If you have a gun, take this advice to heart: get a lock and make sure your children cannot get to it.

School, library and store-related damages also raise different liability. Parents may be liable up to $7,500 for the willful miscon-duct of their children that results in:

- Injury to school employees or other pupils;

- Damage to school property; or

- Damage to personal property belonging to school employees.[29]

Also, the parent or guardian having legal custody of a child who steals merchandise from merchants or books or materials from libraries may be liable for the retail value of the merchandise or fair market value of the books or materials, up to $500.[30]

The trend is to hold parents responsible for the acts of their children. Cities across the nation are enacting laws that will make parents clean up the graffiti their children

---

[24]Civil Code §1714.1
[25]Civil Code §1714.1(b)
[26]*Robertson vs. Wentz* (1986) 187 CA3d 1281

[27]*Reida vs. Lund* (1971) 18 CA3d 698
[28]Civil Code §1714.3
[29]Education Code §48904
[30]Penal Code §490.5

cover our buildings with. So, keep an eye on your children, or you may find yourself with a scrub-brush in hand and minus some cash in your wallet.

I. When is a minor no longer a minor? Emancipation

An emancipated minor is a person under age 18 who is considered to be an adult. To become emancipated, a minor must:

• Enter into a valid marriage, whether or not the marriage is terminated by a dissolution;

• Be on active duty with the U.S. military; or

• Be declared an emancipated minor by a court.[31]

To obtain a court order, the minor must file a petition showing that he or she is at least 14 years old, manages his or her own financial affairs, and lives apart from his or her parent or guardian with that person's "consent or acquiescence." A judge will then decide whether or not to declare the minor emancipated.

Once a minor is emancipated, he or she has most of the same rights as an adult, such as the rights to:

• Consent to medical treatment;

• Enter into a binding contracts;

• Buy and sell real estate;

• Sue and be sued;

• Make a will or a trust;

• Establish his or her own residency; and

• Apply for welfare.[32]

---

[31]Family Code §§7110–7122
[32]Family Code §7050

If the law establishes an age different from 18 for certain activities (such as driving, which is 16, and drinking, which is 21), an emancipated minor must wait until he or she reaches that age before legally engaging in the activity.

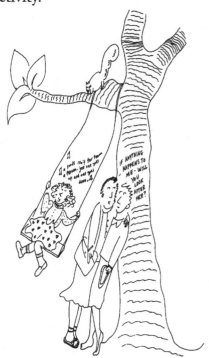

J. Must companies allow parents time off to have a baby or care for a sick child? The Family Leave Act

Yes. Employers with 50 or more employees are required to grant leaves of absence of up to four months to employees who have been with the company for at least one year and who need to take time off to care for a newborn or newly adopted baby, or an ill parent, spouse or child.

When the employee returns, the same or a comparable job must be available. The law also requires that employers let workers on leave continue their health care and retirement benefits, although the employer can insist that the employee on leave pay the group rate.

7

Child rearing by separated parents

As the divorce rate has hovered around 50% for decades, and having children without first being married is no longer rare, it is now a common thing for people to find themselves raising children (their own or their new mate's) whose parents do not live together. There is a huge body of experience available as more and more parents find sane ways to handle the raising of children separately.

Most of the harm from separation and divorce comes from *continued* inability to resolve bad feelings. If you want to help your children heal, resolve all hard feeling about their other parent; get past it, let it go, at least in your own mind.

The law correctly presumes that it is best for a child to have frequent and continuing contact with both parents.[1] But it's not enough that this is the law—it must be made real. Both parents have to keep in mind how much their children need a friendly, relaxed, loving relationship with *both* parents. If you can make it work, it would be the greatest gift you could possibly give your children.

Experience shows that when children are encouraged to have a good relationship with both parents, everything goes more smoothly—visiting, child care, and more regular payment of child support.

It is possible to end a relationship and still maintain a healthy family unit around the children, but it takes commitment, effort and flexibility. That's a small price to pay for your children's well-being.

---

[1]Family Code §3020

A. Who won custody?

If you are asking or answering this question, you are already off on the wrong foot. Children are not property to be won or lost and thinking about things this way will surely lead to trouble. One parent is going to feel cut off and left out. This leads to hurt, resentment, increasing estrangement, and lapses in support payments. This is all very bad for the child. If the other parent of your children is thinking along these lines, send a copy of this book with a marker at this chapter.

Always keep in mind that you will both be the children's parents forever. Nothing can change that. Try to think about things this way and always use words that reflect this coparenting reality.

B. Understanding your custody/visitation order

If you or your spouse have children from a previous marriage (or relationship), you probably have an order from a court defining your rights and responsibilities regarding the children. Here is a little background to help you understand your order.

Terms. The traditional terms, "custody" and "visitation," are losing favor because they encourage parents to think in terms of something to win or lose rather than a child to be cared for. One parent ends up feeling that he or she has "lost" custody and somehow lost contact with the child. This attitude needs to be changed, especially in your own mind. What you are really trying to do is settle child care arrangements when parents no longer live together.

Between yourselves, and in your written agreements, you can use terms like "primary care" instead of "custody." Instead of visitation, you should create a "parenting schedule." Do everything possible to increase the sense of both parents that they are fully and completely the child's parents even though now living separately. You should always use the kinder terms, even though the law still speaks of custody and visitation.

Now for the legal terms: In California, custody has two parts, physical and legal (both are explained below). Either type of custody may be awarded to one parent only—*sole* custody—or to both parents together—*joint* custody. Most child support orders award joint legal custody to the parents with sole physical custody to Mom. California law establishes no preference or presumption in contested proceedings for either Mom or Dad or for sole or joint custody.

Keep in mind, this is an explanation of the legal meaning of custody terms. As a practical matter, when your child is with you, *you* have the care of that child, regardless of whether you have "sole" custody, or are the "custodial" or "noncustodial" parent.

1. Legal custody

Legal custody concerns the rights and responsibilities of a parent to make decisions regarding the health, education and welfare of his or her child. *Joint legal custody* means that the parents will share the rights and responsibilities equally.[2] If you have an order that specifies *joint legal custody,* this means that either parent acting alone can make decisions regarding the health, education and welfare of the child, unless the order

specifies the consent of both parties for any particular kind of decision. Alternatively, "sole legal custody" gives one parent the exclusive right to make decisions affecting the health, education and welfare of the child.[3]

2. Physical custody

Physical custody determines where the child will live. "Sole physical custody" means that the child will live with and be under the supervision of one parent, subject to court's power to order visitation.[4] "Joint physical custody" means that each parent will have significant periods of physical custody (not necessarily 50/50). Custody must be shared in a manner that ensures the child frequent and continuing contact with both parents.[5] "Joint physical custody" does not require that the child spend exactly half his or her time with each parent[6]—it could just as well be 70/30 as 50/50. The order should clearly specify the periods of time each parent will have with the child and give a reasonably detailed schedule for when the child will be with each parent.

[2]Family Code §3003

[3]Family Code §3006
[4]Family Code §3007
[5]Family Code §3004
[6]*Marriage of Birnbaum* (1989) 211 CA3d 1508,1515

Joint custody does not mean equal custody or equal support. Child custody and support, although obviously related, are different legal obligations. For child support purposes, the court considers one parent to be the custodial parent and the other parent the noncustodial parent. Both parents have a continuing obligation to support the child, which means the noncustodial parent almost always has to contribute at least some support, by making payments to the custodial parent. The size of these payments depends upon the relative income of both parents and the needs of the child.

3. Custody and taxes

Each year, one parent can claim the child as a dependent on his or her income tax return.[7] Be sure to get tax advice about how to handle the child exemptions in order to save the most taxes for the family. It usually will pay to have the high earner take them. If the high earner is not the custodial parent, the custodial parent must sign a release each year waiving her right to the exemption.[8]

If the parents have joint custody of only one child and both parents remain single, that means only one parent can claim the child as the basis for a Head of Household filing status. This status is worth big tax savings, so get advice about how to handle the situation to everyones' advantage.

Each parent can deduct the amount expended for a child's medical expenses, regardless of who takes the deduction. For more information, contact your local office of the Internal Revenue Service and ask for the free IRS publication 504, *Tax Information for Divorced and Separated Individuals.*

---

[7]Internal Revenue Code §151(c)
[8]Internal Revenue Code §152(e)(2)

4. Visitation

The parent who does not have the primary care (custody) of the child is almost always awarded some care time to be with the child (visitation rights).

Once, it was common for judges to award "reasonable rights of visitation." Today, this is not considered to be a good idea because no one knows what it means in day-by-day terms. You can't tell when a parent can or cannot visit. These days, most judges want the parents to come up with some sort of schedule, even a general one, that indicates when the child will be with each parent. It is still possible to get *reasonable visitation*, but more detail is preferred.

The best policy is to have a specific visitation schedule, in writing. If you happen to have an order which simply gives one parent "reasonable rights of visitation," we recommend that you work up a *specific* schedule and put it in writing. See Section I.

The law presumes that it is in the child's best interest to have maximum contact with both of its parents. It is therefore very unusual for a judge to deny all visitation between a parent and child. If the evidence shows that contact might endanger the child, a judge is likely to order visitation under supervision rather than deny it completely. It would take clear, strong evidence that any contact at all would endanger the child's physical, mental or emotional health before a judge would order no visitation at all.

5. Visitation for grandparents and stepparents

A court has the power to award visitation rights to a stepparent if that person and a child's natural parent get a divorce. If the natural parent strongly objects, however, a court will be reluctant to grant the visitation.[9]

Courts can also grant visitation rights to a child's grandparents when the parents get a divorce, unless both parents are opposed to it. If the parents disagree about grandparent visitation rights, the issue will be referred to mediation.

Remember, the court's objective is to award custody and visitation rights according to the "best interests" of the child. The court will not award custody or visitation based upon the parents' interests.

C. Parenting plans— Why you should have one

The goal of a good parenting plan is to work out and write down the coparenting relationship and set out a relatively detailed schedule for when each parent will have the care of the child.

Putting your agreement in writing does not imply distrust in any way—it is a practical and sensible thing to do that vast experience has proven to be very valuable. A written plan can help refresh memories if human nature proves true to form and the parents remember the arrangement differently.

A detailed plan helps to create stability and security. It will help settle disagreements if any arise. Parents can depart freely from their agreed plan day-to-day by mutual agreement, but whenever they can't agree on something, they can rely on what the plan says. This is why the plan should be as detailed as possible. If the plan is sufficiently detailed, it doesn't matter very much what terms your order uses because the parenting plan will define in concrete terms what your parenting relationship is and where the child will be at any given time.

At the end of this chapter is an example of a relatively detailed parenting plan that is primarily a *schedule* so you can see what one might look like. A more complete parenting plan could also include terms for how and when parents communicate (can you call each other at work?), decisions which are to be made jointly (schools, medical care, religious training), information to be shared (the teacher called to say Josh is misbehaving), responsibility for child-rearing tasks (who's taking Julie to the dentist), relationships with relatives and stepparents (how often will the kids get to see grandma?).

The plan must be appropriate to the child's age. A plan for an infant will be different than that for a young child and different again when the child becomes a teenager. Yes, this means you will be working out many changes in your parenting plan over your child's life.

Changes should be written down, because a court cannot enforce oral agreements in the

---

[9]Family Code §§3101 et seq.

face of a written one that was made part of an order. A court order always supersedes any oral or written agreements so, ideally, you would make a formal stipulation and change your existing court order to state your current agreement. If you never get around to doing the right way, you'll be in the majority. That's not good; it's not right; but it's the way it is.

D. When things change— Modifying court orders

One thing you can count on is that things will always change and your parenting arrangements will have to change to keep pace. Parents remarry, change jobs, move around. If nothing else changes, the child always will. A schedule for an infant *has* to be different from a schedule for a child and *that* will be different as the child grows through various stages. So get used to the idea that things will have to be adjusted from time to time.

Parents can agree to change court orders regarding children at any time for any reason or no reason at all. An agreed change of orders is called a stipulation, and a stipulated change will always be granted unless the judge who reviews the paperwork becomes concerned that the change may not be good for the child.

If the parties don't agree to a change, either parent can ask the court to modify the order if he or she can show there has been some *substantial change of circumstance* since the last order was made and that it would be in the best interests of the child for there to be a modification.

The change of circumstances may be the age of the child, an increase or decrease in in-

come or expenses, a move, a change in jobs, or a pattern of behavior (for example, if a court finds that the custodial parent has frustrated visitation, this could be considered grounds for a change in the orders).

However, you can't just run into a court and get a judge to settle a parenting disagreement. Read what happens below when you can't settle it yourselves.

E. What happens when parents can't agree?

There are a lot of ways to settle a disagreement short of running to court. You can talk it out (negotiate), or get some parenting counseling or get advice from therapists, friends, relatives or religious leaders. Many communities have parent support groups and family service agencies that you might want to look into.

An excellent way to settle a difference is for both parents to take the problem to a professional family mediator. Mediation is usually very effective in a relatively short time.

Nolo's *Practical Divorce Solutions* has some great information on how to work effectively with your ex-partner. It would be a good read for *both* parents who are having difficulty devising a parenting plan.

If you can't agree and you try to take your parenting disagreement to court, you will first be required to see a court-appointed mediator. This is usually very effective in a limited number of visits and may be one of the best bargains in California. All communications are confidential. However, if the parties do not reach an agreement, counties differ as to whether or not the court mediator will make a recommendation to the judge.

If court mediation doesn't work and you still can't agree, you can put the facts before a judge[10] and let him make a decision. However, you have to understand that most judges do not like to see parenting disagreements in court. They know how bad a court battle is for children and they know that court is not a good forum for settling such issues. Judges have many tools to help parents—or pressure them—to work out a solution on their own.

It is very common for a judge to appoint a psychologist or social worker to visit the parents and the children, do a home study, and make a recommendation which the judge will generally follow. The judge can also order the parties to attend counseling sessions for up to a year and set the proportion in which the parties will bear the cost.

No one wins in a legal battle, but the children and your pocketbook will *always* lose. Battling in court over custody and visitation issues is terribly expensive and not very effective. You put your family's decisions and choices in the hands of a judge who does not really know or understand the personal dynamics of your situation. Do not resort to a court battle unless you have exhausted all other possibilities.

F. Parenting problems and the law

1. Can visitation be restricted or denied?

In general, no. The relationship between parent and child is so protected that courts almost never order no visitation at all. To get an order preventing any visiting at all you must have a very strong case showing that even supervised visits will most likely be very dangerous or detrimental to the child. If you need a court order that prevents all visiting, you should retain an attorney.

You can get an order that visitation be permitted only under supervision if you show "good cause," which means clear evidence of conduct that is dangerous to either the children or the parent, such as abuse of alcohol or drugs, or a history of violence. Supervised visitation means that an adult acceptable to the court is present during the visits with the restricted parent. A court is not allowed to order unsupervised visitation to a person convicted of abusing his child.[11] A mother who has repeatedly attempted suicide and has serious alcohol problems will probably be allowed only supervised visitation. Also, supervision may be required if the noncustodial parent has a history of domestic abuse against the custodial parent.[12]

Prostitution, when brought to the court's attention, is a reason to deny or limit visitation. Homosexuality is not. Religious differences between parents is not a reason to limit visitation unless the tension is clearly harmful to the children. Even where a parent is obviously unfit to take care of children over a long period, courts normally bend over backwards to allow some contact. The court will always make its decision based upon what is in the *best interests of the child.*

If your spouse has a history of harassing and annoying you, word your agreement or orders so you exchange the child in a public place, or design some other plan so that you never have to see your ex-spouse, possibly by arranging exchanges through third persons.

[10]Family Code §3185(a)

[11]Family Code §3030
[12]Family Code §3100

The parent with custody is not entitled to forbid an arranged visitation for any reason other than the well-being of the child. If the visiting spouse arrives in a drugged or drunken state, or any condition that would be dangerous to the child, it would be reasonable to prevent the visit on that occasion. However, visiting cannot be refused because of a disagreement, ill will between the parents, or even because of a complete failure to provide support.

Apart from exceptions like those discussed above, any parent who keeps or conceals a child in order to frustrate custody or visitation orders is guilty of a crime.

Support cannot be suspended because visitation has been frustrated. In extreme cases, however, deliberate and persistent interference with visitation and the parental relationship has led to reduction or termination of support or a switch of custody to the other parent.

The law provides for additional support as compensation to help cover costs for periods when the visiting parent fails to assume caretaker responsibility. Conversely, a parent prevented from exercising visitation rights is entitled to compensation for expenses incurred. A parent who incurs extra expense because the other parent thwarts visitation may request that the court order compensation from the other parent to cover the extra costs.[13]

2. Kidnapping or concealing children

In California, a felony is committed if a person with a right of custody or visitation takes or conceals the child with the intent to deprive the other parent of contact with the child.[14] In addition, a federal law, the Parental Kidnapping Prevention Act (PKPA), provides severe penalties against parents who kidnap their own child.

However, it is a defense if there is a reasonable belief that the child will suffer immediate physical or emotional harm. A pattern of domestic violence, not necessarily in the child's presence, is considered evidence of danger to the child.

If a child is taken or detained by another person in violation of a court order, the district attorney *must* take all actions (civil and criminal) necessary to locate and return the child and the person who violated the order.[15]

If your ex-spouse (or spouse) takes the kids and leaves or threatens to leave the country, there is a procedure whereby a parent who lives in the U.S. and has a valid custody order can deliver to the U.S. State Department's Passport Issuance Office a copy of the custody order; the State Department will then either revoke any passport already issued for the child, or make sure that no passport is issued for the child in the event one is requested by someone other than the custodial parent.

---

[13]*Marriage of Wood* (1983) 141 CA3d 671

[14]Penal Code §277
[15]Family Code §3131

These procedures, however, are often insufficient to prevent international child-snatching episodes. For that reason, in 1988, the United States signed an international treaty, the Hague Convention on Civil Aspects of International Child Abduction. The nations that have adopted the treaty have set up procedures for tracking down children taken outside their countries in the hope of helping to put an end to children being taken from their lawful parent.

If your child has been taken to a different state or country in violation of a court order, or you fear he or she may be, we advise you to *immediately* contact the district attorney's office in your area.

3. Taking children out of the state or country

Many parents fear that they'll be accused of kidnapping their own children if they take them out of the state or country for a trip. Don't worry—you can take your kids anywhere you want unless a court order or custody agreement says otherwise. So take a look at your agreement. Chances are it doesn't mention out-of-state or out-of-country travel. If it does, it probably states that you must notify the other parent in advance before leaving. Be sure to comply with the order. Keep copies of letters you send and make detailed notes of conversations or phone calls.

Always let the other parent know your plans—this will ease anxieties and set the tone for reciprocal behavior in the future.

4. When a parent moves away

Parents are required by law to notify the other parent in writing, at least 45 days in advance, of an intention to change a child's residence for more than 30 days.

As to whether or not a court would prevent a move over the objection of the other parent, the law is complicated and depends to a large extent on the family situation. Generally speaking, custodial parents must consider the child's contact with the other parent before moving, and there must be "compelling" reasons for the move which outweigh the benefit of existing patterns of contact with both parents.

Because a parent is sometimes forced to move for a job or other family reason, courts are reluctant to prohibit a parent from moving. On the other hand, they are equally reluctant to break up a parenting relationship by permitting children to be moved away from a parent they see regularly. Before a move will be permitted, it must be established that it is in the best interests of *the child*.

If there is a move in your future, the best thing you can do is discuss the possible move with your ex, considering what is truly best for the child, and try to reach an agreement regarding the move. Like all other agreements, it should be put it in writing, and signed by both parents.

G. Custody actions in other states

In a highly mobile culture like ours, it is very common for parents to move from state to state. Custody actions could come up in more than one state, and to have more than one court trying to rule on the same case would be a big mess.

To combat multiple-state problems, the Uniform Child Custody Jurisdiction Act[16] (UCCJA) has been adopted by most states,

---

[16]Family Code §§3400–3425

including California. The Act's purpose is to stop courts of different states from rendering separate custody determinations. This is accomplished by requiring any litigation concerning the custody of a child to take place in the state where the child and her family have the closest connection; or where the evidence concerning the child's care, protection and personal relationships is most readily available. Also, in most circumstances the courts of different states will not hear a case regarding the custody or visitation of children where another state has already issued a custody order.

Basically, the UCCJA promotes cooperation among the courts of different states, so that one fully informed custody determination is made that transcends state lines.

So *generally* speaking, if you have a California court order (and you still live in California), another state will not issue a new custody determination.[17] Legally, this is because California has continuing jurisdiction over the custody of the children involved. (Jurisdiction is a legal concept which limits which court has authority to hear a particular case.)

The UCCJA is an important weapon for parents who have custody or visitation problems with an ex who lives in another state. However, it is also complicated legislation, so in order to ascertain your rights, you need the help of an experienced family law attorney.

H. Common questions and answers

Here are some answers to frequently asked questions.

1. Am I responsible for my spouse's child support payments?

Generally speaking, no.[18] The support obligation is considered a debt incurred before marriage and thus the spouse who incurred the debt is alone liable. However, *all* community property may be used to satisfy a premarital debt of a spouse (in the event of a divorce, the community will be entitled to reimbursement; see Chapter 3). If you do not want your earnings liable for your spouse's support obligation, place your wages and earnings in a separate account and do not mix or "commingle" them with other community property—meaning that your spouse can't have access to the separate account.

2. Can my ex change my child's name to that of her new spouse?

A parent may petition the superior court for a change in a minor child's name.[19] If only one parent signs the petition, the petition must specify the address of the other parent, so that he can be notified and appear at the name-change hearing if he wants to object to the change.

---

[17]28 U.S.C. 1738(A)(d)

[18]Family Code §4057.5
[19]CCP §§1275 et seq.

In deciding whether to permit the name change, the sole consideration is the child's best interests. For example, the court will consider the effect a name change will have on preserving the father-child relationship and whether or not having a different name than the mother will be adverse to the child.[20]

3. Who pays for the kids' transportation to visit the noncustodial parent?

It depends on who has more money and who moved away. Try to work out your own compromise.

4. Does the custodial parent have to facilitate visitation?

Yes, the custodial parent is required to take reasonable steps to make visitation possible, such as being generally cooperative and specifically taking the children to the airport or bus station if travel is required. Custodial parents, however, can't be punished if their teenage children refuse to visit the other parent.[21]

5. Can I refuse to pay child support if I'm not allowed to visit?

No. A parent who pays support must continue to make the payments *regardless* of the custodial parent's behavior regarding visitation. The narrow exception to this rule is that if a custodial parent deliberately conceals a child from the noncustodial parent, and then many years later reveals the child's location and tries to collect the child support unpaid all those years, a court may agree that the noncustodial parent need not pay. The noncustodial parent can get his or her visitation rights enforced by the court, however, and can request compensation for money spent in attempting to exercise his or her visitation rights.[22]

[20] *In Re Marriage of Schiffman* (1980) 28 C3d 640

[21] *Coursey vs. Superior Court* (1987) 194 CA3d 147
[22] Family Code §§3556, 3028

I. A sample parenting plan

This plan is relatively detailed. *Do not* simply copy it—think it over, then adapt the details to fit your family and your particular circumstances.

1. *[Mother/Father]* shall be designated as the "Primary Custodial Parent." The Primary Custodial Parent shall have the primary physical responsibility for the children except for *[Mother's/Father's]* parenting time set forth below.

2. Basic Parenting Plan:

   a. **Weekends:** Alternate weekends, commencing _____, from Friday at 6 p.m. until Sunday at 7 p.m. The weekend shall be extended to 7 p.m. on Monday if the Monday is a holiday when the children are scheduled to be with *[Mother/Father]*.

   b. **Weekdays:** Every *[other]* Wednesday, commencing _____, from 4 p.m. to 9 p.m.

   c. **Spring School Vacation:** During the children's spring vacation from school, *[Father's/Mother's]* parenting time shall be from 6:00 p.m. Friday to 6 p.m. Wednesday if his/her regular weekend is *before* the vacation, or shall be from 6 p.m. on Wednesday to 7:00 p.m. Sunday if his/her regular weekend is *after* the vacation.

   d. **Summer School Vacation:** Six weeks during the children's school vacation time during the summer with starting and ending times to be agreed upon by the parties. During these six weeks, the children will spend alternate weekends with *[Mother/Father]* from Friday at 6 p.m. until Sunday at 7 p.m. The weekend shall be extended to 7 p.m. on Monday if the Monday is a holiday when the children are scheduled to be with *[him/her]*.

   e. **Holiday Schedule:**

      Thanksgiving: *In odd-numbered years*, from 6 p.m. on the Wednesday before Thanksgiving until 6 p.m. on the following Sunday.

Christmas: *In odd-numbered years*, from noon on December 26 until 6 p.m. on the day before school resumes in January.

In even-numbered years, from 6 p.m. on the last school day before Christmas school vacation until noon on December 26.

or

Seven consecutive days, including any regularly scheduled weekend time, during the children's Christmas holiday from school. The starting and ending times shall be agreed upon by the parties.

Other Holidays: As agreed by the parties.

3. Each parent shall be responsible for picking up the children at the beginning of his or her parenting time.

4. Either parent may designate any competent adult to pick up the children and to be with the children when they are picked up.

5. Each parent shall give at least 24 hours advance notice to the other parent if he or she must change the schedule. The parent requesting the change shall be responsible for any additional child care costs that result from the change.

6. Both parents will cooperate in finding alternate child care for those periods when regular child care is not available, and the cost of said child care shall be included when the parties establish how the cost of child care is to be shared.

7. Neither parent may remove, or cause to be removed, the minor children from the state of California without 30 days prior written notice to the other parent. This provision applies to vacations *and trips* outside of the state of California.

8. Neither parent may change his or her residence or the residence of the minor children without 60 days prior written notice to the other parent.

8
Is my family provided for?–Estate planning

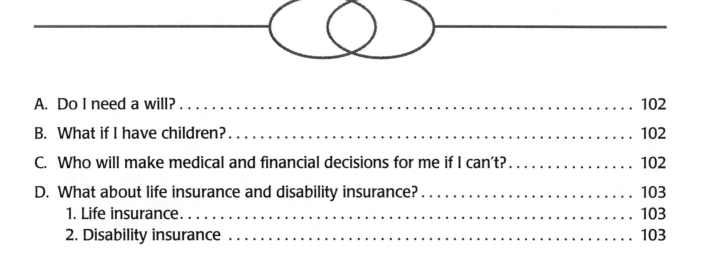

Estate planning (perhaps better thought of as lifetime planning) is a very useful and important step that too few take the time to do. Proper estate planning can ensure that your family is provided for if you die or become permanently disabled. It allows your spouse (or whoever you name) to make medical decisions for you should you become unable to do so. It provides much needed direction for your loved ones when you die. It can be as simple or as complicated as you want it to be. Our goal here is simply to raise the BIG issues you should consider. When you decide to actually *do* something about any of them, you will want to read more in some of Nolo's other books:

Plan Your Estate

Make Your Own Living Trust

Who Will Handle Your Finances If You Can't?

Nolo's Simple Will Book

Power of Attorney Forms Kit

A. Do I need a will?

Yes, especially if you have children. If you should die without a will, the state will distribute your property under a method called "intestate succession." There are literally *no* advantages to dying without a will (or other device that distributes your property on death), so make sure you have one.

B. What if I have children?

Providing for your minor children if you die involves two different concerns. The first concern is who will raise the children if you can't. Children cannot be "willed." This means that you can't leave them to someone to be taken care of. But you can suggest who should care for them if you and your child's other parent should die. To do this, you name that person to be the children's guardian in your will.[1]

When a minor child is left with no living parents, the court appoints an official guardian of the child. Most likely the court will appoint the one you suggested and named in your will, so you and your spouse or ex-spouse should together decide who you would like to have raise your child if something happens and neither of you can do it. Make sure that person is named in *both* your wills. You also want to make sure that the person you name as guardian is aware of your decision and is willing to accept the responsibility.

The second concern is how to provide financial support for your children. (See Section D below.) Because minor children can't own more than a little property outright, an adult must be legally responsible for supervising and administering all property owned by a child. You should name someone in your will to manage your child's property after you die. (Usually it is a good idea to name the same person you named as guardian, but it is not necessary to do so.)

C. Who will make medical and financial decisions for me if I can't?

Too often, health care emergencies find families unprepared. Either because a loved one's wishes are not known, or because no one has the authority to carry them out.

A *durable power of attorney for health care* is a mechanism for giving a particular person the

---

[1]Probate Code §1500

authority to make medical decisions for you if you become unable to give your own informed consent. It allows you to choose a trusted person to carry out your wishes regarding medical care and avoids the need for court action. Likewise, a *financial* durable power of attorney allows you to select a trusted person to handle your finances should you become unable to do it yourself.

How does a durable power of attorney for health care differ from a living will? A living will is a document that states the signer's desire to be allowed to die a natural death and not be kept alive by machines or other artificial means. It has no binding legal effect; rather it serves as an advisory document and a statement of the signer's intentions.

We believe that good estate planning should include a durable power of attorney for health care and finances. Nolo's *Power of Attorney Forms Kit* shows you how to draft a durable power of attorney.

D. What about life insurance and disability insurance?

An important goal of estate planning is to provide ready cash and pay debts, taxes and living expenses for your family. This is especially important if you are the family's main provider.

1. Life insurance

Life insurance can be an important part of estate or lifetime planning. It can be used to supplement an estate which is too small to adequately provide for a family, or it can be used to create an estate, where no other assets exist. Often young couples, who have yet to acquire any real assets, rely on life insurance to provide for the family's support should tragedy strike.

There are several types of life insurance policies, two of which we will describe briefly:

- Term insurance provides a cash payment if one dies within a limited period. When the term expires, there is no cash or other value;

- Ordinary or "whole life" insurance exists for the entire life of the insured, so long as he or she continues to pay the premiums. Whole life insurance generally has a cash value at any given time which the insured can borrow against or receive if the policy is cancelled.

The death of a spouse may create support problems for the family. If you and your spouse do not have sufficient assets to maintain the family should one of you die, life insurance may be a good option for you to consider.

2. Disability insurance

If you are the sole wage earner in your family and you have children to support, disability insurance may also be an option you should consider. Depending upon the policy, it provides a set amount of steady income should you become disabled and unable to work. See your insurance agent for more details.

Don't underestimate the importance of basic estate planning; it allows *you* to make important choices and saves your loved ones worry and expense.

Don't put this off too long. You never know how soon it will be too late.

9
Domestic violence

Domestic violence is the leading cause of injury to women, causing more injuries than muggings, stranger rapes, and car accidents combined.

It is tragic that so many couples who once blissfully bonded together (formally or informally) come to violent blows. FBI statistics reflect this shattering reality: a woman is abused every 18 seconds in our country alone. There are an estimated 28 million battered women in the United States—more than *half* the married women in the country. Although family abuse is certainly not a recent phenomenon, public recognition and concern over the seriousness of the problem is.

Acts of domestic violence occur in households of every race, income level, and education. Everyone from doctors to ministers batter. It is primarily a crime against women and children—but not always.

Words, fists, guns and knives are all used as weapons. None are more hurtful than the other because it is not the bruises and broken bones that paralyze victims; rather, it is the damage done to self-esteem, self-respect and sense of worth that leaves victims damaged and helpless.

Each situation, though different, is strikingly similar. And only one thing needs to happen in each case for the violence, emotional or physical, to stop—the person being abused needs to decide that she will not allow it to happen anymore. Once that commitment is made, financial, legal and emotional help are available to assist you through the process. You can't expect the abuser to the stop the violence—*you* must stop it, by regaining your power and making decisions which will protect yourself and your children.

A. When to get help

The most common type of domestic emergency involves violence. Violence is defined as emotional, physical or sexual abuse inflicted on a person by another. Victims of domestic violence are in need of immediate court intervention to get and keep the abuser out of the house and other places where the victims routinely go (such as work, school and day care), and to prevent future harassment.

The California legislature has attempted to address the problem of domestic violence by enacting a number of laws that allow victims to obtain appropriate court relief—which often means instant relief.[1]

Often, the hardest part of getting help is recognizing and accepting the fact that you need it. If you are in an abusive situation, you need help—there is no shame in being a victim of domestic violence; the shame belongs to the abuser.

In this chapter we will give you an overview of the kinds of protections available and where and how to get them.

B. What kinds of protections are there?

Here's the good news—restraining orders work. If you are in a violent situation, get a restraining order so the police have something to work with in protecting you. The police want to help you, but you have to help yourself first.

Current domestic violence laws are far-reaching when compared to those of only a few years ago. They provide relatively simple procedures a woman can follow, either with

---

[1]Family Code §§6240–6388

or without an attorney, to prevent further violence to her and her family. There is no filing fee to obtain a restraining order and it is something you can do yourself.

In Fall 1995 Nolo Press will release a book about how to get a restraining order.

1. Types of relief

The purpose of the domestic violence laws[2] is to prevent a recurrence of domestic violence and to assure a period of separation for the persons involved. To facilitate these goals, a court is authorized to issue emergency "ex parte" (where only one party tells her side of the story to the judge) protective orders, called Temporary Restraining Orders (TRO). The TRO can:

- Legally restrain the abuser from "contacting, molesting, attacking, striking, threatening, sexually assaulting, battering, or disturbing the peace" of the other household members specified in the order.

- Order the abuser to leave the home, regardless of whether he is the legal owner or renter, and not return to the home unless it is necessary to recover clothing and personal things.[3]

- Order the abuser to keep away from certain places, things or people.

- Determine temporary child custody and visitation rights in both marital and non-marital situations.

In addition, the court has the authority in a TRO to:

- Restrain the abuser from disposing of real or personal property; and

- Determine the temporary use of real or personal property and payment of certain kinds of debts.

The court can also issue the above orders by telephone when court is not in session.[4] A law enforcement officer (policeman, sheriff or even Department of Parks and Recreation officer) must request the order, based on his or her belief that the adult or child is in danger of domestic violence. The officer gets the order orally, writes it down, and then serves it on the party to be restrained. The orders last a few days after being issued, so you need to go to court for a regular TRO and a hearing date as soon as possible. The regular TRO will last until both sides have had a chance to express themselves at a hearing. After the hearing, the court is authorized to make orders that can continue in effect for up to three years and may include any of the following:

- Any of the six "ex parte" orders listed above; and

- An order for child support;

- An order that the abuser pay any household member for any loss (like wages) or out-of-pocket expenses (such as medical costs or temporary housing) incurred because of the violence;

- An order requiring all household members to participate in counseling where the parties agree, intend or continue to live with each other; and

- An order for the payment of attorney fees and costs to the prevailing party.

[2]Domestic Violence Prevention Act; Family Code §§6200 et seq.
[3]This part of the order can be made when the actual or threatened harm is either emotional or physical in nature, and regardless of whether the relationship was marital or nonmarital.

[4]Family Code §§6241, 6250

The court may issue these more permanent orders without first issuing a TRO, when one party sets a hearing and formally notifies the other of the day, time, location and issues; this procedure ensures that each party has an opportunity to present his or her views.

Remember—temporary restraining orders work. If you are in a violent situation, get one. It sends an important message to the abuser that you won't tolerate any more abuse and that society stands behind your decision to have it stop.

 Resist mutual restraining orders. Some judges prefer to issue temporary restraining orders against both parties when one party files papers with the court requesting protection against domestic violence. You should protest this practice (which equates your conduct with the abuser's) and remind the judge that the law allows mutual restraining orders only if both parties appear and show evidence justifying the mutual orders.[5]

2. How do I get a restraining order?

In Fall 1995 Nolo Press will publish a book about how to get a restraining order. Before then, if you need help getting a restraining order and can't afford an attorney, contact one of the various domestic abuse help centers that are found in most communities. Call the Legal Aid office in your area (you will find them listed in the white pages) and ask them for contacts and references. In fact, it is possible that they will help you directly. Ask the County Clerk for the *Instructions for Orders Prohibiting Domestic Violence*[6] booklet, which is helpful for filling out the necessary forms.

3. How long does it take?

Emergency or ex parte orders are usually issued immediately upon filing the proper paperwork (called *Application and Declaration, Order to Show Cause* and *Temporary Restraining Order*) with the County Clerk's office in the Superior Court. At the time the judge grants the ex parte temporary restraining order, a hearing will be scheduled within 20 days so that the other person can tell his side of the story. The exact procedure for obtaining the judge's signature and hearing varies from county to county. The County Clerk's office or a women's support center will have this information.

Any temporary restraining order granted at this hearing can last up to three years unless the court shortens or lengthens the time or unless both parties agree to an extension.

4. Will I have to go to court?

Yes, you will have to attend a hearing. The hearing will usually take place in a regular courtroom, open to the public. This can be very intimidating for an abuse victim, who will now have to confront the abuser in public. Fortunately, most court personnel are

---

[5]Family Code §§6320, 6305

[6]Cal. Rules of Court, Rule 1296(a)

sensitive to this and try to make you feel as secure as possible. More importantly, you have the right to have a "support person" be with you at the table during the hearing and accompany you to mediation if there is a custody or visitation dispute.[7]

When your case is called, you have to explain why the defendant (abuser) should be restrained. This will usually be the same explanation you gave in the *Declaration* that accompanied your *Application* for the TRO, but you may also introduce additional facts. Once you complete your presentation, the defendant has a right to tell his side. No matter how much you believe he is lying, you must prevent yourself from reacting while he is testifying. You will be given a chance to speak again when he is finished.

Both you and the abuser have a right to ask each other questions (cross-examination). If you become extremely upset by this process (many people do), take what time you need to compose yourself—ask the court for a recess if necessary. If you feel you are being mistreated, say so. The judge will lean over backward to protect you.

When both you and the abuser have been heard, the judge will ordinarily decide the case right there, usually in favor of the victim, and extend the TRO (now called a temporary or preliminary injunction) for an indefinite period. Or, the judge may modify the terms of the TRO in accordance with the testimony. Judges almost never remove all restraints in the face of testimony showing that domestic violence has occurred.

5. What if he violates the order?

If the abuser knowingly and willfully violates a court's order, he has committed a misdemeanor punishable by a fine of not more than $1,000 and/or imprisonment in the county jail for not more than one year.[8] Each county handles the situation differently, so call your local police department to find out their policy.

 Even though over 85% of restraining orders work—a piece of paper is not the same as real protection. It's a mistake to think that a piece of paper which says you are protected from violence is the same as real physical protection. If there is a real fear for physical safety, a confidential change in physical location is likely to be of more immediate help than a restraining order. Only you know what your spouse or partner is capable of. Don't leave yourself or your children exposed to real physical danger.

---

[7]Family Code §6303. You can also request meeting separately with the mediator instead of being in the same room with the abuser. And, if visitation with the abuser is ordered, the court may order that it must be supervised by another adult.

[8]Penal Code §§273.5, 273.6

C. Spousal rape

The essential guilt of rape consists in the outrage to the person and feelings of the victim. Any sexual penetration, however slight, is sufficient to complete the crime.[9]

Society is beginning to change its notion of rape from that of a sexual act to that of a violent act. As in so many other instances where there is an evolution in societal values, laws concerning rape have been amended to reflect the change. For example, in many states, cross-examination of a rape victim on her previous sexual history is forbidden, and definitions of rape have been modified to be gender-neutral so that both males and females can be victims of rape.

In California, spousal rape is a crime.[10] Previously, courts and legislatures were reluctant to deviate from the ancient rule that a husband was immune from the crime of raping his wife. But, in the wake of growing concern over the large number of married women in this country subjected to abuse by their husbands, and in the recognition that rape is a violent act, the crime of rape in California is now defined to include:

- The act of sexual intercourse when a wife resists, but her resistance is overcome by force or violence; or

- The act of sexual intercourse when a wife is afraid to resist because of her husband's threats of great and immediate bodily harm.

There can be no arrest or prosecution on a charge of spousal rape, however, unless the violation is reported to the proper authorities within 90 days. This 90-day reporting requirement appears to have been included because of the fear on the part of lawmakers that charges of rape would be used months later as a weapon in divorce.[11]

D. Recoveries for interspousal injuries

In California, one spouse can sue the other for injuries inflicted deliberately or as the result of negligence, just as if the spouse were a stranger. If you have an abuser spouse who has regular income, property (like his share of the family home), or liability insurance, you should seriously consider a suit for damages.

Personal injury damages recovered by one spouse for an injury inflicted by the other spouse are separate property of the injured spouse. This is the rule whether the injury occurs prior to marriage, during marriage, prior to permanent separation or after permanent separation.

E. Some common questions

1. If I call the police, what will happen to my spouse?

Your safety and the safety of your children must be your primary concern. Having said that, if your spouse has violated a restraining order in force or has otherwise battered or harassed you,[12] and the police are called, here's what will happen. A statement will be taken from you, and your spouse (or whoever the abuser is) will be arrested and taken to the police station. Depending on his record and the circumstances, he may or may not be granted bail (if he was already on probation for another violation, he will kept

[9]Penal Code §263
[10]Penal Code §262

[11]Penal Code §262
[12]Penal Code §646.9(d)

in jail for at least 48 hours).[13] The District Attorney's office will decide whether there is enough evidence to press charges and will usually want you to testify against your spouse.

What about firearms? A sheriff or police officer may, at the scene of an incident of domestic violence involving a threat to human life or a physical assault, take temporary custody of any firearm in plain sight or discovered in the course of a search consented to by one of the occupants of the residence. A gun or other firearm so seized cannot be released for at least 48 hours, but must be released within 72 hours. Also, a person subject to a restraining order may be ordered to refrain from owning, possessing or purchasing a firearm while the protective order is in effect.[14]

2. I have no money—where can I go?

Many times a woman and her children are in immediate physical danger and common sense dictates that they get away from the physical presence of the abuser (or potential abuser) as quickly as possible. In the past, one reason women failed to do this is that they had no place to run. Consequently, California has enacted legislation that provides funding for shelters for women and children in this situation. The locations of the shelters are not made public in order to protect the victims and staff. Battered women's shelters unfortunately pass in and out of existence frequently. To locate a battered women's shelter or program near you, call one of the organizations listed in Section G below.

The police have an obligation to provide a written notice to victims of domestic violence that informs them:[15]

- How to obtain information about available shelters;

- How to obtain information about other domestic violence services in the community;

- That the victim has the right to ask the district attorney to file a criminal complaint against the abuser;[16] and

- That the victim has the right to petition the civil court for various protective orders.

If you have children. Is a battered woman who takes her kids and goes into hiding guilty of child concealment or kidnapping? Not if her case fits one of these two situations:

- a) She gets protective orders first, authorizing her to take custody of the children and denying the abuser visitation. Emergency orders are available by telephone with the aid of a law enforcement officer where the parent and child are in imminent danger.

- b) She has "good cause" to take the kids and run—a reasonable belief that it is necessary to protect the child.[17] But you must file a report with the law enforcement agency where the child had been living within a reasonable time (your address will remain confidential).

---

[13]Penal Code §243(e)
[14]Penal Code §12021(g)

[15]Penal Code §13701; Family Code §6389
[16]When a person "presses charges" against another, they are really requesting that the district attorney's office file charges. In California, as in most states, only the district attorney, city attorney and state attorney general can actually file criminal charges against a person.
[17]Penal Code §277

If you do run off with the children, we strongly recommend that you get a court order either before you go or very soon afterward.

Before a court will permit the abuser to visit with the children (when the danger is likely only to the spouse), it is first *required* to consider whether the circumstances require that visitation be supervised (where third persons are present), or whether visitation should be suspended or denied entirely. If visitation is permitted, the court is *required* to specify the time, day, place and manner the transfer of the children is to occur for visitation purposes, in order to ensure the safety of all family members[18]

3. What should I do ?

If you are in an abusive situation, start gathering information about who can help you and where to go for help. If you are in immediate danger, call 911. Call any of the organizations listed in Section G below; call your local police department; call a local shelter. They will help you end the abuse in a safe manner. Do not allow domestic violence to be your children's inheritance or your legacy.

You are not alone, and there is help available. We repeat: the hardest part is recognizing and accepting that you need help.

F. Nonviolent emergencies

There are a number of potential situations affecting divorcing or quarreling husbands and wives (or nonmarital partners) that do not involve violence or the need for temporary custody arrangements, but that still give rise to the need for emergency orders from a judge. Nonviolent emergencies include:

- **Child-snatching within state.** You have come home from work to find that your spouse has left and taken the children to another place in California.

- **Child-snatching to another state.** You and your spouse had worked out a custody and visitation schedule but, over the weekend when she had the kids, she left California and said you'll never see the kids again.

- **Left high and dry.** You don't work outside the home (and didn't during the marriage). Now that you've separated, he refuses to support you, has closed the joint accounts, and you have no other source of income.

- **Children need support.** Although you are able to meet most of the children's financial needs, you can't meet them all. Your spouse, from whom you're separated, refuses to provide any assistance.

- **Assets need protection.** Your spouse left last night; you have good reason to believe that she is going to empty the community bank accounts and that she will cash in other community assets.

- **Foreclosure of your home is threatened.** Your spouse left about three weeks ago and refuses to contribute toward the mortgage or other monthly bills. You're afraid the bank is going to start foreclosure proceedings pretty soon.

Even if your situation is not precisely one of these just listed, if you're experiencing a domestic emergency of some similarly pressing type, you may be a prime candidate for an ex parte or other type of temporary protective order. As a reminder, an ex parte order is issued by a judge at your request without the

---

[18]Family Code §§3031, 6323

other person (party) being present. In this section, as with the last, we give you an overview of when and how these orders can be obtained, but for detailed instructions, you will want to get Nolo's book on domestic abuse and other restraining orders. This book will be available in Fall 1995.

1. I need help today—Ex parte orders

An ex parte order can be sought in each of these three situations.

- Child-snatching within state;

- Child-snatching to another state (see Chapter 7); or

- Assets need protection.

It may also be appropriate if foreclosure of your home is threatened. Here's a brief description of how ex parte orders are obtained in these situations.

You must fill out three forms (called *Application and Supporting Declaration, Temporary Restraining Order* and *Order to Show Cause*), all available from the County Clerk. If the request is to keep your spouse from emptying the bank accounts or taking other community property, another form called a *Property Declaration* must also be completed. If custody is involved, a *Uniform Child Custody Jurisdiction Act (UCCJA) Declaration* may need to be filled out. If the child has been taken out of state, you will need a lawyer.

You deliver the filled-out forms to the judge for her signature. If a foreclosure of your home is threatened, the other side must be notified before delivering the forms to the judge. A telephone call is enough. Child-snatching or asset protection would not require this prior notice, as they fall within exceptions to the notice requirement. Notice

is not necessary when it would be futile to do so or unduly burdensome under the circumstances, or when it would defeat the purpose of the order.

When the judge signs the papers, she grants a temporary order which usually lasts only a few weeks. She also schedules a hearing to be held within 20 days. At that time, the issues raised in the ex parte order are addressed by both sides.

The emergency or ex parte order is not enforceable until it is *properly* served on your spouse. If your spouse has taken off with the kids and you don't know where she's gone, the district attorney's office may be able to help (see Chapter 7).

After the papers have been served, there is an enforceable order. If there's a violation of the order before the scheduled hearing, the court has the power to declare your spouse in contempt of court and, depending on the violation, throw him in jail. At the hearing, the judge will decide whether to make the ex parte order remain effective. Chances are that if the other party has done something fairly nasty and the judge fears he or she will do it again, the judge will make the order permanent.

2. I need help soon—Non–ex parte orders

Non–ex parte orders should be sought in these situations at what's called an Order to Show Cause hearing:

- Left high and dry;

- Children need support; or

- Foreclosure of your home is threatened.[19]

---

[19]An ex parte order generally would not be sought with a foreclosure or other debt problem, because if the bank is threatening foreclosure there are a whole lot of steps it must take before the actual foreclosure can occur, which means it is not an emergency situation.

Briefly, here is how it works:

You fill out two forms (called *Order to Show Cause* and *Application for Order and Supporting Declaration*). If the request is for support, payment of debts, or any other financial issue, an additional form (called an *Income and Expense Declaration*) with its attachments, also must be completed.

The next step is to call the Clerk to set up a hearing date. Then, as with the ex parte order, the *Order to Show Cause* must be delivered to the judge for her signature. No notice to the other side is necessary because she is just being ordered to appear in the courtroom and tell her story.

The papers are then filed at the courthouse and served on your spouse. A hearing is held at the time and place indicated in the papers and both sides have an opportunity to tell their story. The judge then determines whether the requested order should be granted.

G. Organizations that will help you get out of a violent situation

Remember, only you can stop the violence. A lot of help is available if you will just call on it.

To find a local women's center or shelter or support group, call your local police department, legal aid office, or district attorney's office. If you belong to a religious group, talk to your minister, priest or rabbi. If you are too embarrassed to talk to your own minister, go to the competition.

You can also call on one of these national organizations. They may have information on groups near you.

National Coalition Against Domestic Violence

P.O. Box 18749

Denver, CO 80218-0749

(303) 839-1852

Serves as an information and referral center for grassroots shelters and service programs assisting battered women and their children.

Woman, Inc.

(415) 864-4722

Maintains a 24-hour hotline.

Battered Women's Justice Project

206 W. 4th Street

Duluth, MN 55806

(800) 903-0111

Focuses on battered women and the criminal justice system; supplies information to attorneys, advocates and battered women.

10
Divorce—How to reduce pain and cost

In the past, divorce was considered a failure, but in today's changed world, it seems to have become a common part of growing up.

Even the nicest marriages sometimes come to an end, and endings are always hard. A change on this scale can't help but affect you in powerful ways. On the positive side, separation or divorce offers you an opportunity for growth; and, while the divorce process can be extremely difficult, research shows that most people are glad they did it a short time after it's over. We are not divorce advocates, but we are open to the idea that spending one's life with more than one person can be a good alternative to spending one's life in an unhappy relationship.

A. Is the marriage really over? Alternatives if you're not sure

You or your spouse are the only people who can answer this question. If one spouse decides it is definitely over, then it is definitely over for both. But, if you are not certain about it, there are alternatives to divorce that allow couples time to work out their problems without breaking the bonds of matrimony:

Trial Separation. Sometimes a trial separation can provide a cooling-off period that helps to settle your emotions and clear your thinking. It gives you a comfortable situation from which to think about and work on reconciliation.

If you are concerned about your spouse mismanaging community funds or assets, a trial separation may not be a good idea unless you can make arrangements that will put that worry to rest. In any case, you have to make practical arrangements for bill paying and child care. Legally, however, there is nothing to be done—just go ahead and separate. Good luck.

Be sure to read Section Q below before arranging a trial separation.

Counseling. Sometimes the intervention of a third party can help bring about better understanding and reconciliation. Consider getting the help of a marriage counselor, religious advisor, or other professional who is qualified to help you and your spouse sort out your problems. Counseling can help spouses communicate more effectively with one another, thus allowing problems to be better defined and more easily understood and resolved. Marriages can be saved if both parties want to work at it.

Divorce counseling is also widely available and we highly recommend it, especially if you have children. In this case, the idea is not to get back together, but to separate decently.

Family Conciliation Court Services[1] are provided by the county. The program is designed to help preserve the family unit and protect the interests of minor children. Essentially, they assist spouses in a reconciliation and settlement of their domestic problems. Some form of conciliation court service is now available in most counties. How does it work? Generally, either you or your spouse file a *petition* (which basically means a request) for conciliation[2] with the court in your area and then you and your spouse meet privately with trained counselors who will try and help you both to resolve the

---

[1]Family Code §§1800–1842
[2]Family Code §1831

controversies that threaten your marriage. These services are available and free of charge to families with children, or families vulnerable to domestic violence.

After a petition for conciliation has been filed, neither spouse may file for divorce for at least 30 days after the conciliation court hearing.[3] If you are interested in this program, call the Superior Court in your area and ask the Clerk for more information.

Whatever decision you make, remember that it takes *two* willing spouses to repair a broken marriage. You can't do it alone.

B. Two ways to end a marriage

If you decide to end your marriage, there are only two ways to dissolve the bonds of matrimony: nullity, and dissolution (divorce). A legal separation will get you separated under court orders, but it does *not* end the marriage. In any of these actions, the court can make orders on property, children, support, and keeping the peace.

A nullity (formerly called annulment) wipes the marriage from existence. It returns the parties to a single status, as if the marriage had never happened. The courts will only grant a *nullity* in very limited circumstances, such as where the marriage was technically void or entered into due to fraud.[4] Because the grounds for nullity are more complex than for dissolution and since courts tend to be more strict in granting one, we recommend you get advice before deciding to try to get one. Call a local family law attorney, or call Divorce Helpline (Section I below).

Legal separation gets the spouses separated and makes orders about children, support and property, but the parties remain legally married. That can sometimes make things a little confusing for creditors who think they can go after the spouse of a debtor, and this is why it takes extra care to insulate separated spouses from future responsibility for each other's debts. If you get a judgment of legal separation and later decide you want to be divorced, you have to start an entirely new action, pay new filing fees, and go through the paperwork to get a judgment of dissolution.

Legal separation is useful to couples who can't divorce for religious or moral reasons but also can't continue to live together. There are a few practical situations where a legal separation works better—where sizable Social Security benefits, veterans' benefits, retirement, or other benefits may be lost if there is a divorce, or where a long-term spouse with an illness or disability may be able to stay on the employed spouse's health insurance (call the plan to see if they allow this).

Divorce in California courts is called "dissolution," as in "dissolving the bonds of matrimony." A dissolution will usually serve your purposes as well or better than either of the other forms. It is clear, final, easier to understand, and the legal formalities are relatively easy to get through—it's the emotional part that's so hard.

Throughout the rest of this chapter, we talk about divorce, but almost every word applies as well to couples getting a legal separation.

C. Three keys to a sane divorce

Divorce can be difficult under the best of circumstances, but it is also very easy to

---

[3]Family Code §1840(a)(b)
[4]Family Code §2210

make it worse. If you go uninformed and unprepared into a divorce, it will be an accident if it does *not* turn into a horrible and horribly expensive nightmare. It doesn't have to be that way if you take a little time to prepare.

Be informed and be prepared. The only way you can avoid the blind path that leads to an uncontrolled divorce is by becoming informed and prepared. It isn't hard and the results are worth it. People who know what's going on invariably get better divorces than those who do not.

If you are going through a divorce, the biggest help you can give yourself would be to read Nolo's book, *Practical Divorce Solutions*. It is a prize-winning guide for making the passage smoother and with less cost. Get a copy for your spouse, too. This is important, because shared ideas work far better than unilateral ones.

Control your case. A Connecticut study (1976) showed that of couples with lawyers, about 60% worked out *all* their own terms without resort to their attorneys, meaning that in most cases the clients do most of the real work anyway. More important is a study in New Jersey (1984) showing that *client control of divorce negotiations is the most significant predictor of a good post-divorce outcome.* "Good outcome" includes things like better compliance with agreements, less chance of litigation, increased goodwill, better coparenting. This means that whether or not you use a lawyer, if you control your own case you will save money, reduce aggravation, and feel good about being in charge of your own life.

Taking control does not mean you can't get help or seek advice; it means that you prob-ably do not retain an attorney. You take responsibility for knowing what's going on and for making your own decisions. You become an active participant in the negotiations. You take responsibility for your own actions and feelings. That's healthy and that's what works. Our *Divorce Helpline* service (Section I) was designed with this idea in mind. Attorneys there will help you without having to be retained. They won't "take" your case.

Keep business and personal matters separate. Many aspects of getting through a divorce are businesslike in nature: money, property, procedures, negotiation and agreements, lawyers and taxes. It is ancient wisdom that business and personal/emotional matters do *not* mix well. The best way to protect yourself, to reduce conflict and confusion, is to keep business matters as separate as possible from emotional and personal concerns. This does not mean that you don't deal with personal and emotional matters—just not at the same time you are taking care of business.

D. A unique opportunity for the spouse who decides to divorce

The primary cause of conflict in divorce is lack of mutuality in the decision to divorce. In other words, both spouses haven't accepted the idea that there is going to be a divorce.

Ideally, the decision to divorce is arrived at together. This does not mean that one spouse may not be sadder or more distressed than the other, but that both come to accept the divorce as the best thing under the circumstances.

In almost every case, however, one spouse works his or her way through to the difficult decision to get a divorce—this person has thought about it, read about, sought advice about it, and processed the emotional pain to reach a decision. Once the decision is made, the decision is finally asserted to the other spouse as a final decision.

The first spouse is now ready to move forward while the other spouse is still wallowing in denial and resistance. The second spouse hasn't had (or taken) the time needed to process the reality of divorce. He or she is in some kind of emotional upset—hurt, fear or anger—and is not ready to discuss details or work out accommodations. This is not a good time to push along on the divorce, even though the first spouse is ready and highly motivated to do so. Moving along too quickly at this point is the root cause of a lot of trouble to follow.

The first spouse to decide to divorce is in a unique and powerful position to affect the future tone of the divorce. By being abrupt and insensitive, you can almost guarantee a bitter, expensive divorce. If you want to encourage a sane resolution of divorce issues, be patient, be sensitive, but most of all, slow down. Give your spouse time to process the changes. Work with your spouse until you can both accept the fact that going your separate ways is ultimately best for both of you.

E. Forces that create conflict

To reduce conflict, you have to avoid or overcome the forces that create it. There are four or five in every case:

1. Emotional upset and conflict: This is about high levels of anger, hurt, blame, and guilt—a very normal part of divorce. If one or both spouses are upset, you can't negotiate, have reasonable discussions or make sound decisions. Complex and volatile emotions become externalized—attached to things or to the children. When emotions are high, reason is at its lowest and will not be very effective *at that time*.

2. Insecurity, fear, lack of confidence, unequal bargaining power: You can't negotiate if either spouse feels incompetent, afraid, or that the other spouse has some big advantage. Divorce is tremendously undermining; it tends to multiply any lack of self-confidence and self-esteem. Also, there are often very real causes for insecurity: lack of skill and experience at dealing with business and negotiation, and lack of complete information and knowledge about the process and the marital affairs. It doesn't matter if insecurity is real or reasonable; it *is* real if it *feels* real.

3. Ignorance and misinformation: Ignorance about the legal system and how it works can make you feel uncertain, insecure and incompetent. You feel as if you don't know what you are doing . . . and you are right! Misinformation is when the things you think you know are not correct. Misinformation comes from friends, television, movies, even from lawyers who are not family law specialists. It can distort your expectations about your rights and what's fair. It's hard to negotiate with someone who has mistaken ideas about what the rules are. Fortunately, both conditions can be easily fixed with *reliable* information.

4. The legal system and lawyers: The legal system is one of the most insidious contributors to conflict and expense in divorce cases.

The legal system is by nature *adversarial*; it is based on the principal of conflict; one side struggles against the other, trying to win. If you retain an attorney to "take" your case, you will probably be dragged into the legal system and this is not what you want in a divorce. Lawyers cannot help you talk to your spouse rationally or overcome the emotional upset, but are rather likely to reinforce it.

In all but the most conflicted divorces, you want to avoid the legal system as much as possible and—with the help of Nolo's books and other services—you can. Unless you are facing immediate threat of harm to yourself, your children or your property, it would be better if you do not *retain* an attorney. Read *How to Do Your Own Divorce* first.

5. Real disagreement: These are the real issues that you want to deal with rationally and negotiate with your spouse. Real disagreement is based on the fact that the spouses now have different needs and interests. After dealing with the first four obstacles, these real issues may turn out to be minor, but even if they are serious, at least they can be negotiated rationally.

The solutions are in your hands: Apart from the legal system—which you can avoid—all obstacles to your agreement are personal, between you and your spouse and between you and yourself. The solutions to your problems are entirely in your own hands and the legal system has little to offer compared with the potential for harm, and especially compared with all the things you can do for yourself outside the legal system.

Take care. Pay special attention to emotional upset and especially insecurity and fear. These are the forces that drive people into a lawyer's office. You want to avoid doing anything that might increase the upset and fear of either spouse.

- The upset person is saying, "I can't stand this, I won't take it anymore! I'm going to get a lawyer!"

- The insecure person is saying, "I can't understand all this, I can't deal with it, I can't deal with my spouse. I want to be safe. I need someone to help me. I'm going to get a lawyer."

This is how cases get dragged into unnecessary legal conflict.

F. How to reduce pain and cost

There are very practical and effective things you can do to deal with the forces described above. They may not all be of use in every case. Use what applies to you.

1. Make some "new life" resolutions: Start thinking of yourself as a whole and separate person. You may feel wounded, but you are healing and becoming whole and complete. Keep that picture in mind. Pain and confusion is part of healing. Let go of old attachments, old dreams, old patterns that don't work; this is your chance to build new ones. Decide you will not be a victim of your spouse or the system or yourself. You will not try to change or control your spouse— that's all over now, it doesn't work, it's contrary to the meaning of divorce. Concentrate on yourself, especially on your own actions. You can do something about what your spouse does by changing what you do. Take responsibility for yourself: if anyone hurts or upsets you, try to understand how you let them do that. Try to become quiet and calm. Keep your life as simple as possible.

2. Insulate and protect your children:
Involving children is going to upset the spouses and harm the children. Keep them well away from the divorce. Tell them the truth in simple terms they can understand, but otherwise, don't discuss the divorce in front of them. Don't pass messages through them. Don't let them hear your arguments or hear you criticize their other parent. Let them know you both love them and will always be their mother and father, no matter what happens between you. Help them understand that loving their other parent is not a betrayal of you; they shouldn't have to choose sides. Help them establish a new pattern of stability so they feel safe, and help them have as much contact as possible with both parents.

3. Get safe, stable and secure, just for a while: Your first and most important job is to do *whatever* you have to do to arrange short-term safety, stability, and security for yourself, the children, and your spouse—in that order. This doesn't mean forever, just for a month or a few months at a time. Don't be concerned yet about the long term or the final outcome, and we're talking about minimum conditions here, not your old standard of living. Don't even try to do anything else until minimum conditions are met. You can't negotiate if you don't know where you will live or how you will eat, or if you are afraid for your safety or if you think your house is about to be foreclosed or your car repossessed. You can't negotiate if your spouse is not in a safe and stable situation, too.

If you can't get both spouses stabilized, the fear and the upset level will go up and you will probably end up in court with attorneys arguing over pretrial motions. Your case will get dragged into the legal system, fighting in court at a very early stage. These legal procedures are tremendously upsetting and *very* expensive, on the order of tens of thousands of dollars for each side. To avoid this kind of outcome, you have to help each other even if you don't feel like it.

4. Agree on temporary arrangements: It takes a long time for things to settle down and for the spouses to work out a final agreement. Meanwhile, you have to arrange for the support of two households on the same old income, the parenting of minor children, making payments on mortgages and debts, and so on. Ideally, arrangements for such things will be set out in writing.

If you can work out your own temporary arrangements during separation, neither spouse will need an attorney to get temporary court orders. Start by agreeing that you want a fair result and will both act fairly. Agree to communicate before doing anything that will affect the other spouse or the estate or the children. The goal here is to avoid surprises and upset. Among other things, that includes closing joint accounts or starting legal actions.

5. Slow down, take some time: If you can make your situation safe and stable for a while, you don't have to be in a hurry. Think of divorce as an illness or an accident; it really is a kind of injury, and it takes time to heal. You have to go slow and easy. Some very important work goes on during this slowdown. You work on reducing emotional upset—this takes time. You work on mutual acceptance—this takes time. You work to help both spouses become confident, stable, secure. Use this time to get reliable information and advice; find out what the rules are.

6. Get information and advice: First, organize your facts, records and documents. You'll want lists of assets, deeds, statements, account numbers, income and expense information, tax returns and wage stubs. Get information from your records and from your accountant, from recent tax returns, and from your spouse. Spouses should have a full and open exchange of information; it helps to build trust and confidence—and it's the law, so you might as well just go ahead and do it. If information is not exchanged freely outside of the legal system, you will probably end up in court with attorneys doing very expensive discovery work.

You should learn the rules as they apply to your case. Read Nolo's best-seller books, *Practical Divorce Solutions* and *How to Do Your Own Divorce*. Make sure your spouse has a copy of these books, then maybe you can discuss some of the issues and ideas in them.

Be very careful where you get advice. Your friends and relatives will be a fountain of free advice, *but don't take it*—the price is too high if they're wrong. They mean well, but probably don't know what they're talking about. Don't take advice from paralegals or people who run typing services; they're not trained for it. You can call Divorce Helpline attorneys (Section I) for practical, settlement oriented advice.

7. Focus on needs and interests; don't take positions yet: A position is a stand on a final outcome: "I want the house sold and the children every weekend." In the beginning, there's too much upset and too little information to decide what you want for an outcome and, besides, positions are a set up for an argument: the other side either agrees or disagrees. It's better to think and talk in terms of needs and interests. These are more basic concerns: "I want what's fair and what the rules say is mine; I need to be secure and have enough to live on; I want to know what I can count on for living expenses; I want maximum contact with my children; I need to get out of debt, especially on the credit cards; I want an end to argument and upset." Put this way, these are goals that you and your spouse can discuss together.

8. Stick with short-term solutions: Concentrate on short-term solutions to immediate problems, like keeping two separate households afloat for a few months; keeping mortgages paid and cars from being repossessed; keeping children protected, secure, stable, in contact with both parents. These are things you can possibly work on together.

9. Minimum legal activity: You want to avoid any legal activity unless it is necessary—zero is best, or the minimum required to protect yourself or just get your case started. Ideally, you will avoid retaining an attorney and you won't give your spouse any reason to retain an attorney.

10. Get help if you need it: For yourself or your children, consider counseling or therapy. For help with talking to your spouse, consider couples counseling or go see a mediator. These low-conflict professionals can help with emotional issues, defusing upset or, in the case of the mediator, with making temporary arrangements.

G. Children of divorce

If you have children, be sure to also read Chapter 7, "Child rearing by separated parents."

Studies show that harm to children is more closely related to conflict *after* the divorce. Everyone has conflict before and during a divorce, but if you want to help your children, get finished with the conflict and resolve it, at least within yourself.

Children need their relationship with both parents. There is a bonding that cannot easily be replaced by a surrogate parent or stepparent. To protect the essential parent-child relationship, you have to insulate children from your own conflict with their other parent. The divorce is not their problem; it's yours. Being a bad wife or husband does not make your spouse a bad parent. So, don't hold the children hostage—they are not pawns or bartering pieces in your game. In the area of custody and visitation, don't bargain with your spouse on any other basis than what will give your children the most stability and the best contact with both parents.

The worst thing for the child of a broken home is feeling responsible for the breakup and feeling that loving one parent is a betrayal of the other. These feelings cause children intense stress and insecurity. To protect your child from almost unbearable pain, don't say anything bad about the other parent in front of the child; don't undermine or interfere in any way with the child's relationship with or love for the other parent; don't put the child in a position of having to take sides. Do encourage every possible kind of constructive relationship your child can have with your ex-mate. Let the children know that you are happy when they have a good, loving time with their other parent.

Kids can really get on your nerves at a time like this and single parenting is enough to overwhelm any normal person. You are not Superman or Mary Marvel and kids are not designed to be raised by one lone person. You need help and support and you need time off from the kids. Make a point of getting help from family, friends and the many parent support groups and family service agencies throughout California. Get references to groups in your area through temples, churches or social service agencies.

H. Can you do your own divorce?

Yes! You *can* do your own divorce. Since Nolo's *How to Do Your Own Divorce* was first published, millions of Californians just like you have done their divorces without retaining lawyers, so you can almost certainly do it too.

You *should* do your own divorce. The legal process—and the way attorneys work in it—tends to cause trouble, raise the level of conflict and greatly increase your expense. No one should *retain* an attorney in any divorce case unless it is absolutely necessary.

There are a few cases where you should *not* do your own dissolution. You should retain an attorney if there is an immediate threat of harm to you or your children, or if your spouse is trying to transfer valuable assets. You may need help if your spouse is on *active* military duty and will not sign a waiver.

I. Who can help?

Books: *Practical Divorce Solutions* gives you practical advice about getting through the emotional, practical and financial obstacles that you face. It's about how to deal with your spouse, how to negotiate, and how to keep your divorce sane.

How to Do Your Own Divorce is about the laws of property, children and support. It tells you the rules and what judges normally do, then it shows you how to fill out the forms to get a divorce.

These best-sellers may save you tens of thousands of dollars and lots of pain. Get a copy of each book and copies for your spouse, too. Share information works better. It will be the best money you ever spent.

Friends, relatives and "common knowledge" are the worst and most expensive sources of advice. Use friends for moral support, but when they give you advice, just smile, say "thank you," but do *not* take it seriously. If you didn't get it from a *current* Nolo book or a family law specialist attorney in California, *don't trust it!* Just because you like or trust someone doesn't make them right. If you take bad advice, who pays the price? You do—perhaps for the rest of your life.

Paralegals act as a typing service for people doing their own divorces—you tell them exactly what you want and they type up the forms and handle the secretarial work. We introduced this innovation in legal service in 1972 and paralegals have since changed the face of the legal map. Their rates are generally $300 to $500 for doing your basic paperwork.

It is very important for you to understand the limitations of paralegals. Some paralegals are trained, but no license, training or other qualifications are necessary—anyone can do it. You *can't* get reliable legal advice from paralegals, nor can they safely prepare your marital settlement agreement (MSA) unless you have a *very* simple case, very little property and use the MSA in Nolo's *How to Do Your Own Divorce*.

There are many good paralegals out there, but you should be careful who you hire—just as when hiring a lawyer or a mechanic. Ask how long they have been in business and be sure to check their references. If you know *exactly* what you want and have no legal questions, no problems, and no MSA beyond the one in *How to Do Your Own Divorce*, then an experienced and reliable paralegal is a very good way to get your paperwork done.

Lawyers who *specialize* in divorce know a lot that could help you, but, because of the way the system works and the way lawyers work, they will almost certainly cause you unnecessary conflict and expense. Do not retain an attorney unless there's no other choice. Getting information and advice from attorneys is tricky, too, because they don't want to help you help yourself, they want to take your case and represent you.

Attorneys will frequently do the first interview for a fairly small fee, but too often they spend that time convincing you that you need them to handle your case. Hourly rates can run up to $400, but $190–$210 per hour is average. Most attorneys require a retainer, about $1,200 is typical, but the amount doesn't matter because the final bill will almost certainly be *much* higher. Few attorneys will give you a definite maximum figure for the whole job. You are doing *very* well if you end up spending less than $2,500 *per spouse* on the *simplest* case; the average in LA and Orange counties when both spouses are represented is over $18,000 *per spouse!*

Divorce Helpline was created to change the way attorneys practice in divorce cases, to provide expert support for people who are doing their own divorces.

Divorce Helpline attorneys work exclusively on solving problems and settling divorces. We will not litigate or represent people—we don't believe in it. Instead, we serve as your guide and assistant. Divorce Helpline attorneys are trained in mediation and communication, and are good at solving problems in a practical way. We have to be, because—unlike other attorneys—we earn *less* if you can't settle your case. If you can't settle, we will refer you to a litigating attorney in your area and give you a refund for any work that was not completed due to your unresolved conflict.

Divorce Helpline can do a much better job for you when we do the *whole* case—the paperwork and the marital settlement agreement—as well as giving you advice. That way we have *all* the information, not just the small bit you are asking about. When we do the whole case, we often find issues, problems to solve and ways to save money that people didn't know to ask about.

Divorce Helpline charges $950 for paperwork, which includes a marital settlement agreement drafted by our attorneys. Using a lot of counseling and most of our other services, it is *possible* to run up a bill as high as $1,500 or even $2,500—your *total* cost for *both* spouses—but the higher costs are quite unusual.

J.   Grounds for Divorce

California is a "no-fault" divorce state—fault is irrelevant when seeking a divorce. You don't get more property or support no matter how bad your spouse was. The idea behind no-fault is simple: a court shouldn't encourage partners to drag each other through their past bitterness and broken expectations. No-fault divorce has been a valuable reform and has worked well.

To be eligible for a divorce in California you must allege one of the following grounds:[5]

- Irreconcilable differences have caused the irremediable breakdown of the marriage; or

- A spouse is afflicted with incurable insanity.

Almost everyone files under the first ground because incurable insanity is hard to prove, whereas irreconcilable differences exist just because one spouse says so.

K. Can you stop your spouse from getting a divorce?

No, you can't stop a divorce. A court will not consider evidence as to the existence or nonexistence of the "irreconcilable differences." If one spouse says there are irreconcilable differences and the other says there aren't, that dispute constitutes an irreconcilable difference and the divorce will be granted. Of course, you want to make sure you get a fair deal, but if you simply try to obstruct a divorce, you will guarantee that some attorneys will make a lot of money. Much of the added cost comes out of your own pocket and the divorce will go through anyway. Obstruction ends up hurting yourself and your children for no gain.

L.   What is a divorce about?

Before you can complete your divorce, you have to settle these issues:

- How to divide whatever property and debts have accumulated during the marriage; and

---

[5]Family Code §2310

- If there will be spousal support; if so, how much and for how long.

If you have minor children, you must also decide:

- How the parents will share the care and responsibility of raising the children; and

- How much will be paid for child support.

As far as the law is concerned, this is what a divorce is about—property, children and support. It doesn't matter whether you do it yourself or an attorney does it, you still have to gather your own facts and make your own decisions.

How to Do Your Own Divorce tells you what the rules are and how things are normally done. It helps you make your decisions, then shows you how to get your case through the courts.

California has a history rich in lawsuits and legislation, one result being that our marital property rules are extensive and detailed. While a lawyer can always use this detail to pick a fight, it is rarely worth it. With few exceptions, one can predict with reasonable certainty what a judge would decide in almost any marital property dispute. There is nothing to be gained by going through costly litigation when almost any problem you could possibly have has already been legislated and litigated.

This makes it possible and very attractive for couples to settle marital property issues through negotiation rather than litigation. Family resources should be split between the partners to a marriage rather than between the partners in a law firm.

M. Full disclosure—it's the law!

In order to get a divorce in California, both spouses must fill out and exchange *Declarations of Disclosure* listing all their property and debts and detailing all income and expenses. Before you enter into a final agreement for support or division of property, each spouse must give the other a *Final Declaration of Disclosure*. These documents need not become public information, because they are not filed with the court, but you *do* have to prove that they were exchanged. Regarding finances, you must be completely honest and open with your spouse because it's the right thing to do—and because it's the law. Any property or information you conceal or mistakenly overlook can come back to haunt you long after you think the divorce is final.[6]

N. Marital settlement agreements

Once you have gathered all the facts and records and understand the rules of property, children and support, the next step is to work out a marital settlement agreement (MSA) with your spouse. *How to Do Your Own Divorce* has a sample MSA that you can use as a guide.

If you have no children, little property and few debts, it's possible to do your divorce without an MSA, but agreements have many advantages and cases with agreements are easier to do, so most people will want one.

No one is pretending that negotiating with your spouse during a divorce is easy; it's not.

---

[6]Family Code §§2104–2105

That's why we wrote *Practical Divorce Solutions*. It has extensive advice about how spouses can get past upset and conflict to negotiate an agreement.

Here's why it's worth a lot of time and effort to get a good, well-drafted marital settlement agreement (MSA):

- Your MSA actually becomes your judgment, so the spouses get to decide everything rather than some stranger (the judge).

- With an MSA you can get far more depth, detail, flexibility and protection than you can get in a judgment with no MSA.

- Once you sign, your divorce is essentially done except for red tape and paperwork.

- With an MSA, you probably won't have to go to court; without one you almost certainly will.

- Most important, divorces that are settled by good agreements usually work out better afterward. Spouses are more likely to comply with terms, have better post-divorce relationships, better coparenting, faster healing, and it just feels better.

Money and more. Often, a lot of money can be gained or lost depending on how things are handled in your MSA, especially where major assets, debts or support are involved. Careful planning, problem-solving and drafting can save thousands or tens of thousands of dollars.

Making an MSA that works: An MSA is different from other contracts. When you sign a contract, you are bound by its terms from that instant. It is not easy for one party to back out or change the terms without the written consent of the other party. However, with a marital settlement agreement, it is

much easier for one party to back out. Any time within one year, one party can go to court to set aside the agreement based on duress or mistake of law or fact. Based on fraud, perjury, or lack of full disclosure, the MSA may be subject to attack for many years.

Attacks against the agreement are limited more by practical considerations than legal ones. It costs a great deal of money and even more in emotional determination to conduct a legal battle. This means your risk increases with the amount of money in your estate *and* the amount of upset in your divorce.

If you want to get on with your life and not have your divorce become a career, it is more important than ever to work for a fair resolution of all issues, emotional and financial, that satisfies both sides. Be open, fair and temperate in all dealings with your spouse; listen more than you speak; don't argue. If necessary, use mediation and even counseling or therapy. Make sure you have a *very* high quality marital settlement agreement. If you have enough income or property to make an attack worthwhile, it is *not* a good idea to write your own or use a paralegal.

Getting a good agreement does not mean getting a signature on the dotted line. The value of your agreement lies in the thought and discussion that leads to it. A good MSA will be thought out, talked out, and negotiated in depth and detail by the spouses. All facts will have been disclosed and both spouses will have had access to every document and record. The agreement must be very carefully drafted.

The three before's. If you get help, be sure to get your information and advice *before* you state your position to your spouse, *before* you draft your MSA, and *before* you sign anything. Afterward will be too late.

Get help? If you need help working things out, read Nolo's books or call Divorce Helpline. We can help with suggestions, problem solving and negotiating techniques. If you live in Santa Clara or Santa Cruz counties, we can mediate in person; in other parts of California, we can do very effective telephone mediation or we can refer you to a family law mediator in your area.

O. What you do to get a divorce

1. Residency: To file for a divorce either you *or* your spouse must have lived in California for at least six months and in the county in which you file for three months prior to filing the papers.

To obtain a legal separation in California, there is no residency requirement nor any six-month wait for it to become effective.[7]

2. Court costs: If you do your own divorce, the cost to file a petition for divorce is from about $182 up to $235. To comply with disclosure laws, there may be a Response fee of an equal amount. We are trying to get changes in the law to eliminate the use of the Response fee for disclosure documents. Finally, there will be photocopy and postage costs, and you will probably want a copy of *How To Do Your Own Divorce* ($21.95) and *Practical Divorce Solutions* ($14.95).

3. How long does it take? The divorce itself is separate from the issues of property, children and support. Assuming you have settled all your issues and there is no contest, a Judgment can be obtained fairly quickly, say two or three months, depending on the

speed of the Clerk's Office in your county. Once the Judgment is entered, all orders become effective immediately and the issues of property, children and support are settled. However, the earliest date the bonds of matrimony can be dissolved is six months from the day the Petition is served on the Respondent spouse. That's the earliest you can get remarried and that is the date the IRS uses to decide if you were married or not in a tax year.

You can get a legal separation as quickly as you can complete your paperwork and get it through the system; a matter of weeks, if you rush it along.

4. Getting it started: Several forms must be filed to get a divorce. They are set out in *How to Do Your Own Divorce*, along with the instructions necessary for filling them out. Meanwhile, here's how the process works.

The person starting the divorce (the "Petitioner") files forms called the *Petition* and *Summons*. The *Petition* lists the issues to be decided. The *Summons* is a message from the court to the Respondent (the spouse receiving the *Petition*). It states that a *Petition* has been filed and if no *Response* form is filed within 30 days, the court may grant what the Petitioner has requested.

5. Serving the papers. The Petitioner must have another person mail or hand-deliver divorce papers to the Respondent. This person can be anyone at all over 18 who is not a party to the divorce. Service is usually easy because most Respondents accept the papers when the couple has discussed divorcing. If the Respondent avoids service, you may have to hire professional help. The details are discussed in *How to Do Your Own Divorce*.

---

[7]Family Code §§2320–2321

6. Automatic restraining orders. Once the Summons is served, both parties are bound by automatic restraining orders that are in effect until the Judgment is entered. Both spouses are ordered not to:

- Remove a child of the parties from the state without prior written permission of the other spouse or order of the court;

- Transfer, sell or encumber (borrow against) *any* property except in the usual course of business or for necessities;

- Cancel, transfer or borrow against any insurance (including life, health, auto, disability) held for the benefit of either the other spouse or a minor child.

7. Mandatory mediation. If you and your spouse have a dispute about child custody or visitation, you *must* be referred to court mediation.[8] That usually works, but if it doesn't, the judge is likely to order a home study by a psychologist or social worker who will then make a recommendation to the court. It is far better if the parents settle rather than let the decision be made by strangers. Over 90% of all custody disputes are settled before trial.

8. Full disclosure: In every case, spouses must exchange full details about their financial affairs. See Section M above.

9. Getting the Judgment. If there is a marital settlement agreement, you can almost always complete the case by mail; no court hearing will be required. A judge can reject the paperwork if there is something wrong with the forms or if the judge is uncomfortable with the agreement and wants testimony on some point, but this is rare.

If you have no agreement or if a hearing is required by the court, don't worry—divorce hearings are relatively easy and won't take more than a few minutes (once your case is called). *How to Do Your Own Divorce* contains a complete script for what to say. Hundreds of thousands of people have successfully represented themselves in court and navigated through hearings on their own.

10. Judgment of Dissolution. The Judgment sets orders that settle issues of property, children and support. It also states the date for the termination of the marriage.

Even after it is issued, a Judgment is not effective until it has been entered in the records by the Clerk. You are also not divorced until the date for termination of marriage that is stated on the Judgment has passed. You would be amazed at how many people think they are divorced, but are still married because they forgot to get a Judgment properly entered.

11. Summary Dissolution. The Summary Dissolution procedure[9] in California is a simplified divorce process that requires only a couple of forms; the *Petition, Preliminary*

---

[8]Family Code §3170

[9]Family Code §§2400–2406

Declarations of Disclosures and the *Request for Final Judgment & Notice*—and no court appearance. You can only use this simplified form if you meet the following qualifications:[10]

A Summary Dissolution must be filed before your fifth wedding anniversary. Both spouses must sign a Petition and you *must* prepare and sign a property agreement unless there is absolutely *no* property and *no* debts to be divided. Both spouses must give up all rights to spousal support. When you sign the Petition, you and your spouse are taking an oath by which you swear that:

- Both spouses have read and understood the Summary Dissolution Booklet (go get one; it's free from the Clerk's office);

- One spouse has lived in California for at least six months and in the county in which you file for at least three months immediately before the date you file your Petition;

- There are no minor children and the wife is not pregnant;

- Neither spouse has *any* interest in *any* real estate *anywhere* in the world;

- There is less than $5,000 in community debts, not counting car loans;

- There is less than $25,000 in community property, not counting cars; and,

- Neither spouse owns over $25,000 separately, not counting cars.

Still interested? If you can meet these requirements you can use the Summary procedure. There is a waiting period of six months after you file your Petition. After that, either

spouse may file a simple form requesting the final Judgment. Unless and until the final Judgment has been requested and entered, there is *no* divorce.

Revocation: At *any* time before the Judgment is requested, either spouse can file a simple form revoking the proceeding, killing it dead. If this happens, a divorce will not take place unless someone starts over with the longer regular dissolution procedure. Because divorce is a time when people often play emotional games with each other ("I'll revoke the whole thing if you don't stand on your head"), be sure that both spouses are serious about getting a Summary Dissolution before you start.

P. Pre-divorce planning and checklist

Nolo's *Practical Divorce Solutions* has a whole section of forms that will help you get your information organized. Gather information from records and from your accountant, from recent tax returns, and from your spouse.

☐ Get organized. Keep all your paperwork neatly in a safe place.

☐ Make a list of all assets.

☐ List all accounts and numbers.

☐ Get copies of deeds, bank and account statements, tax returns and wage stubs.

☐ Gather detailed income and expense information.

☐ Check all insurance policies to see how children and ex-spouses will be affected by separation and divorce.

☐ Contact pension plans and get a copy of the plan booklet and summary statements of the employee's account.

---

[10]Family Code §2400

☐ Consider a written agreement setting out how current joint obligations are going to be paid during the divorce process.

☐ Before you separate, get credit cards and open bank accounts in your own name. Arrange with your spouse to close all joint accounts.

☐ After you separate, verify all joint accounts have been closed. Also make sure your ex is paying the creditors he or she agreed to pay. If payments aren't made, you'll get stuck with the bill.

Health Insurance

☐ Investigate health insurance after divorce or separation. Spouses may no longer be eligible for coverage under their ex-spouse's health insurance. However, under the federal COBRA (Consolidated Omnibus Budget Reconciliation Act of 1986) law, if your former spouse's employer has at least 20 employees and offers group health insurance, you have a right to continue health insurance at the group rate for a period of up to 36 months following final decree of the divorce. The cost may seem to go way up because the employer's share is no longer applied for you. You have only 60 days from the day the divorce becomes final to deliver a written notice of the divorce to the health plan administrator stating that you want to continue with their plan.

☐ Call the plan or the employer's personnel department and find out what the coverage is and what the cost will be after the divorce. Then call other plans and shop around for a better deal. If you have a pre-existing illness, you will almost certainly need to stay with the old plan.

Taxes

☐ Get information on tax issues. Call your local IRS office and ask for copies of their free publications:

555: *Community Property and the Federal Income Tax*

504: *Tax Information For Divorced or Separated Individuals*

929: *Tax Rules for Children and Dependents*

596: *Earned Income Credit* (for low-income people)

☐ Decide how you will file your next tax return. The IRS considers you married for the tax year if your marriage was not terminated by December 31. You might get a better tax rate if you file jointly, but you are then each responsible for the income and tax liability of the other, and you have to arrange a fair way share in any tax bill or refund. You might want to talk to a tax accountant about this.

☐ Think about who will receive the tax exemption for the children.

☐ If you have large assets, like a family home, get information about tax consequences of keeping it, selling it and what happens, taxwise, to the spouse who moves out.

☐ Temporary spousal support payments based on an informal agreement may not be deductible unless you get a court order for it. The support paid then becomes taxable income to the recipient.

Insurance, wills, estate planning

☐ A divorce or separation will automatically revoke all existing bequests to a former spouse and remove the former spouse as executor under any will made before the judgment. If the parties intend the former spouse to continue as a beneficiary or executor, a new will must be made.

☐ The judgment will *not* remove a former spouse as beneficiary under life insurance policies. This is something you may want to cover in a marital settlement agreement. Contact the carrier if you want to change your beneficiary.

☐ Note that once a Summons has been served, beneficiaries or terms of insurance policies can not be changed until after Judgment has been entered.

☐ If you have children, you should consider naming a guardian in your will.

Q. When the separation date becomes very important

Everyone knows (or can find out) exactly when they got married, but it's a lot harder to say exactly when you separated. This is because separation is a state of mind.[11] Separation is more than just living apart; it is that point in a marriage when "spouses have come to a true parting of the ways with no present intention of resuming marital relations." Just because a husband and wife live in separate residences, this by itself doesn't determine that they are separated. Just because they live in the same residence doesn't prove they were *not* separated. We realize this sounds strange, but what the courts are looking for is conduct that demonstrates a final break in the marital relationship; conduct which manifests the *intention* of ending the marriage.

In most cases, it won't matter exactly when you were separated. Just use any reasonable date and go on about your business. However, there are cases where the date you separated can make a big financial difference.

The separation date affects the character of both income and debts. After the date of separation, any property acquired by one spouse is the separate property of that spouse and any new debts are separate as well.

Example

On the night of Jerry and Elaine's 20th wedding anniversary, Jerry tells Elaine that he is moving out because he is not happy in the marriage. Jerry moves into an apartment and soon his new girlfriend joins him. Jerry continues to have dinner with Elaine at their home two or three nights a week, and she often accompanies him to business dinners and holiday parties. In addition, Elaine continues to do Jerry's laundry once a week. Elaine still hopes she and Jerry will get back together. This scenario continues for about two years, at which time Jerry seeks a divorce from Elaine, so that he can marry his girlfriend Muffy.

Jerry wants the separation date to be the date he moved out of the family home, nearly two years ago (then his earnings during the move-out period will be his separate property). Elaine argues that the separation date is the date Jerry filed for divorce. The court holds that since Jerry and Elaine held themselves out as a married couple (business dinners, etc.), and since Jerry accepted the "wifely" contributions of Elaine, no intent to dissolve the marriage occurred until Jerry actually filed for divorce. Thus the court held that all property accumulated from the time Jerry moved out until the time he filed for divorce is the community property of the marriage, and owned equally by both spouses.[12]

---

[11] *Marriage of Baragry* (1977) 73 CA3d 444; *Marriage of Imperato* (1975) 45 CA3d 432

[12] *Marriage of Baragry* (1977) 73 CA3d 444

The example illustrates how important the separation date can be. You have to pay special attention where one of the spouses might earn large commissions on sales or might get a big bonus or employee stock option. For such people, the date of separation might mean a great deal.

Spouses who separate and then reconcile several times may have more than one period during their marriage where property acquired is the separate property of one spouse rather than the community property of the marriage.[13]

Our advice: if you separate for a trial period and intend that any accumulation of property during that separation be the separate property of the acquiring spouse, get it in writing. If you think your separation is permanent, write it in a letter to your spouse and keep a copy.

R. Working on an agreement— How to negotiate with your spouse

1. Get information and advice: Use the Nolo Press books, *How to Do Your Own Divorce* and *Practical Divorce Solutions.* Give your spouse these books. Call Divorce Helpline and talk to one of our consulting attorneys who will help you develop options.

2. Be prepared: Get the facts about your assets, debts, incomes and expenses and help your spouse get the facts, too. Make sure you understand the rules that apply to your facts.

3. Be businesslike:

- Keep business and personal matters separate.

- Meet in a neutral place where you can be free of interruptions.

- Make appointments with each other; be on time; make an agenda ahead of time.

- Be polite and insist on reasonable manners in return. If things become un-business-like, ask to set another date to continue the discussion.

4. Problem solving: Approach your negotiations as problem-solving sessions—something you work on together.

5. Balance the negotiating power.

- If you feel insecure, become informed, be well prepared, use an agenda, get advice and guidance from Divorce Helpline. Don't feel pressured into responses or arguments; state your ideas, listen to your spouse, think it over until the next meeting. Then get advice if you want it. Don't continue if you aren't calm or if the meeting doesn't stay businesslike. Consider using professional mediation.

- If you are the more confident spouse, help build your spouse's confidence so he or she can negotiate confidently. Share all information openly. Be a super listener. Restate what your spouse says to show you've heard it. Don't respond immediately, but take time to think about what you've heard. Tone yourself back: state your points clearly but don't try to persuade or repeat yourself. Listen, listen, listen.

6. State issues in a constructive way: Instead of, "I want the house," say, "The house is very important to me because . . ." The second statement encourages discussion and negotiation.

7. Build agreement: Start with the facts and don't go forward until you both agree to the

---

[13]*Pattillo vs. Norris* (1976) 65 CA3d 209

facts about your property, income, expenses, and debts. Write down facts you agree on and facts you do not agree on. Do research and exchange documents to resolve differences. Compromise. Make a list of issues you do agree on. Try to refine the issues you do not agree on and make them more clear and precise.

8. Be patient and persistent. It takes time for people to accept new ideas and adjust their thinking. Don't be in a hurry; don't be surprised at upsets and reversals. Things will almost always resolve themselves later.

9. Get help: If you feel that your case is blowing up, don't give up. That is exactly the time to call Divorce Helpline. Helping people negotiate and settle differences is what we do best. It goes much better if we get involved with your case as early as possible, but it's never too late to try.

10. Mediation: When you and your spouse have come to an impasse on an issue or a group of issues and need a guide to help you find your way, a good mediator may be the right prescription. You can call Divorce Helpline for mediation. They work with you in person if you are convenient to San Jose or Santa Cruz. More frequently, they do mediation by telephone.

When you look for a professional mediator, choose one who is also a family law attorney. Non-attorney mediators do not feel comfortable working with the legal issues in a divorce. The best way to find a mediator is to get a recommendation from someone you trust.

Mediation is not marriage counseling, and is not used to get back together with your spouse. You should look at mediation as a positive step taken to resolve your disagreements that will help direct you and your spouse toward a fair divorce settlement.

Divorce Helpline—(800) 359-7004

We created Divorce Helpline to provide legal support for people who are doing their own divorces or related legal procedures. At Divorce Helpline, you work with a team of experienced, top quality family law attorneys. We guide you through your case with reliable information and advice, counseling, problem solving, negotiation and mediation. We can draft your agreement, value pensions, do all the paperwork and handle the red-tape. We are expert at helping you solve problems, settle issues, and negotiate agreements.

Divorce Helpline serves all of California by phone, mail and fax. If you are near our offices in San Jose and Santa Cruz, you can come in personally. Our fixed rates for services are among the lowest for attorney assisted divorce. Call for more information about how we can help you.

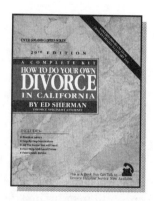

Berkeley

The Living Together Kit, by Attorneys Toni Ihara & Ralph Warner $17.95

A detailed guide designed to help unmarried couples understand the laws that affect them. It contains comprehensive information on estate planning, paternity agreements, living together agreements and buying real estate. Sample agreements and instructions are included.

How to Change Your Name, by Attorneys David Loeb & David Brown $19.95

All the forms and instructions you need to change your name in California.

A Legal Guide for Lesbian and Gay Couples

by Attorneys Hayden Curry , Denis Clifford & Robin Leonard $21.95

Laws designed to protect married couples don't apply to lesbian and gay couples. This book shows you how to write living together contracts, plan for medical emergencies and plan your estates. It also covers domestic partner benefits and the practical and legal aspects of having and raising children. Includes forms and sample agreements.

The Guardianship Book, by Lisa Goldoftas & Attorney David Brown $19.95

Thousands of children in California need legal guardians because their parents have died, abandoned them or are unable to care for them. This book provides all the forms and instructions needed to obtain a legal guardianship without a lawyer.

How to Adopt Your Stepchild in California

by Frank Zagone & Attorney Mary Randolph $22.95

This book provides step-by-step instructions and all the forms necessary to complete an uncontested stepparent adoption in California.

Nolo's Simple Will Book, by Attorney Denis Clifford $17.95

It's easy to write a legally valid will using this book. With instructions and forms, you can name a personal guardian for minor children, leave property to minor children or young adults and update your will when necessary. It also contains an up-to-date discussion of estate planning basics with information on living trusts, death taxes and durable powers of attorney.

WillMaker 5.0 $69.95

DOS / Mac / Windows

WillMaker, the most trusted and comprehensive will program available makes writing a will easy. Leading you step-by-step in a question and answer format, WillMaker customizes your legally valid will, and allows you to print it and sign it in front of witnesses. WillMaker comes with a 200-page manual which provides all the legal and practical information you need to do the job right. Good in all states except Louisiana.